EZEKIEL, DANIEL, & REVELATION

GOG OF THE LAND OF MAGOG, THE
KINGS OF THE NORTH & SOUTH, &
THE EIGHT KINGS OF REVELATION

EDWARD D. ANDREWS

EZEKIEL, DANIEL, & REVELATION

GOG OF THE LAND OF MAGOG, KINGS OF THE NORTH AND SOUTH, & THE EIGHT KINGS OF REVELATION

Edward D. Andrews

Christian Publishing House
Cambridge, Ohio

Copyright © 2019 Christian Publishing House

All rights reserved. Except for brief quotations in articles, other publications, book reviews, and blogs, no part of this book may be reproduced in any manner without prior written permission from the publishers. For information, write, support@christianpublishers.org

Unless otherwise indicated, Scripture quotations are from the Updated American Standard Version of the Holy Scriptures, 2019 edition (UASV).

EZEKIEL, DANIEL, & REVELATION: GOG OF THE LAND OF MAGOG, KINGS OF THE NORTH AND SOUTH, & THE EIGHT KINGS OF REVELATION

ISBN-13: **978-1-949586-77-0**

ISBN-10: **1-949586-77-4**

CHAPTER 1 Authorship of Daniel and Revelation Defended

Daniel Misjudged

You have a critical body that has formulated an opinion of the Bible, especially prophetic books, long before they have ever looked into the evidence. The liberal critical scholar is antisupernatural in their mindset. In other words, any book that would claim to have predicted events hundreds of years in advance are simply misrepresenting itself, as that foreknowledge is impossible. Therefore, the book must have been written after the events, yet written in such a way, as to mislead the reader that it was written hundreds of years before.

This is exactly what these critics say we have in the book of Daniel. However, what do we know about the person and the book itself? Daniel is known historically as a man of uprightness in the extreme. The book that he penned has been regarded highly for thousands of years. The context within says that it is authentic and true history, penned by Daniel, a Jewish prophet, who lived in the seventh and sixth centuries B.C.E. The chronology within the book shows that it covers the time period of 616 to 536 B.C.E., being completed by the latter date.

The New Encyclopædia Britannica acknowledges that the book of Daniel was once "generally considered to be true history, containing genuine prophecy." However, the *Britannica* asserts that in truth, Daniel "was written in a later time of national crisis—when the Jews were suffering severe persecution under [Syrian King] Antiochus IV Epiphanes." This encyclopedia dates the book between 167 and 164 B.C.E. *Britannica* goes on to assert that the writer of the book of Daniel does not prophesy the future

INTRODUCTION

The first chapter will defend the authorship of Daniel and the time of his writing the book. It is imperative that the reader study this chapter. Why? Because Daniel either wrote the prophetic apocalyptic book that bears his name in the sixth century B.C.E. before the time of his prophecies, meaning that he is a legitimate prophet of God; or another fraudulent author penned the book in the second century B.C.E., which would be after most of the prophecies of the book, meaning it is simply repeating historical facts as prophecies.

The second chapter is an introduction on how a reader is to interpret a prophetic book based on the conservative, evangelical the historical-grammatical method of biblical interpretation (objective), as opposed to the liberal to moderate the historical-critical method of biblical interpretation (subjective). Chapters 3-6 cover the battle between the kings of the south and the kings of the north. While this will eventually culminate into a discussion of the United States of America, it is important that you take note of the kings of the south and the north beforehand, to see how detailed Daniel is in his prophetic message. Chapter 8 will cover what role the United States has played in the last days and how the election of Donald J. Trump as president was timely.

CHAPTER 7 Babylon the Great, the Beast, the Seven Kings, and the Eighth King of Revelation.................... 101

    Revelation 17:1-18 (the Last Days) 101

CHAPTER 8 Donald Trump as President of the United States, what Does This Mean for Christians? 113

    The United States in Bible Prophecy? 118

    How Do True Conservative Christians View Voting? 119

Bibliography... 123

Table of Contents

INTRODUCTION 1

CHAPTER 1 Authorship of Daniel and Revelation Defended 2

    Daniel Misjudged 2

    Evidence that Revelation Is Authentic and Inspired 32

CHAPTER 2 Interpreting Prophecy 37

    The Prophetic Judgment of Nineveh 37

    Supposed Unfulfilled Prophecy 40

    Prophetic Language 43

    Interpreting Prophecy 45

    Grammatical Aspect 46

    Historical Aspect 47

CHAPTER 3 The Kings of the South and the North 51

    Daniel 11:1-9 (530 – 226 B.C.E.) 51

CHAPTER 4 The Kings of the South and the North 60

    Daniel 11:10-20 (226 – 175 B.C.E.) 60

CHAPTER 5 The Kings of the South and the North 66

    Daniel 11:21-35 (175 – 164 B.C.E.) 66

CHAPTER 6 The Kings of the South and the North 85

    Daniel 11:36-45 (the End Times) 85

    Who is Gog of the Land of Magog Mentioned By Ezekiel the Prophet? 97

but merely presents "events that are past history to him as prophecies of future happenings."

How does a book and a prophet that has enjoyed centuries of a reputable standing, garner such criticism? It actually began just two-hundred years after Christ, with Porphyry, a philosopher, who felt threatened by the rise of Christianity. His way of dealing with this new religion was to pen fifteen books to undercut it, the twelfth being against Daniel. In the end, Porphyry labeled the book as a forgery, saying that it was written by a second-century B.C.E. Jew. Comparable attacks came in the 18th and 19th centuries. German scholars, who were prejudiced against the supernatural, started modern objections to the Book of Daniel.

As has been stated numerous times in this section, the higher critics and rationalists start with the presupposition that foreknowledge of future events is impossible. As was stated earlier in the chapter on Isaiah, the **important truth for the Bible critic is** the understanding that in all occurrences, prophecy pronounced or written in Bible times meant something to the people of the time it was spoken or written to; it was meant to serve as a guide for them. Frequently, it had specific fulfillment for that time, being fulfilled throughout the lifetime of that very generation. This is actually true; the words always had some application to the very people who heard them. However, the application could be a process of events, starting with the moral condition of the people in their relationship with Jehovah God, which precipitated the prophetic events that were to unfold, even those prophetic events that were centuries away.

However, it must be noted that while Daniel and Isaiah are both prophetic books, Daniel is also known as an apocalyptic book, as is the book of Revelation. This is not to say that Isaiah does not contain some apocalyptic sections (e.g., Isa 24–27; 56–66) What is assumed by the critical scholar here is that there is a rule that a prophet is understood in his day, to be only speaking of the immediate concerns of the people. They are looking at it more like a proclamation, instead of a future event that could be centuries away. Before addressing this concern, let us define apocalyptic for the reader:

Apocalyptic

This is a term derived from a Greek word meaning "revelation," and used to refer to a pattern of thought and to a form of literature, both dealing with future judgment (eschatology).

Two primary patterns of eschatological thought are found in the Bible, both centered in the conviction that God will act in the near future to save his people and to punish those who oppress them. In prophetic eschatology, the dominant form in the OT, God is expected to act within history to restore man and nature to the perfect condition which existed prior to man's fall. Apocalyptic eschatology, on the other hand, expects God to destroy the old imperfect order before restoring the world to paradise.

Origins of Apocalypticism

In Israel, apocalyptic eschatology evidently flourished under foreign domination.

From the early 6th century B.C., prophetic eschatology began to decline and apocalyptic eschatology became increasingly popular. The Book of Daniel, written during the 6th-century

B.C., is the earliest example of apocalyptic literature in existence.[1]

The problem with the modern critic is that he is attempting to look at the Biblical literature through the modern-day mindset. His first error is to believe that a prophetic book was viewed only as a proclamation of current affairs. The Jewish people viewed all prophetic literature just as we would expect, as a book of prophecy. The problem today is that many are not aware of the way they viewed the prophetic literature. While we do not have the space to go into the genre of prophecy and apocalyptic literature extensively, it is recommended that you see Dr. Stein's book in the bibliography at the end of the chapter.

Some Rules for Prophecy

- One needs to identify the beginning and end of the prophecy.
- The reader needs to find the historical setting.
- The Bible is a diverse book when it comes to literary styles: narrative, poetic, prophetic, and apocalyptic; also containing parables, metaphors, similes, hyperbole, and other figures of speech. Too often, these alleged errors are the result of a reader taking a figure of speech as literal, or reading a parable as though it is a narrative.
- Many alleged inconsistencies disappear by simply looking at the context. Taking words out of context can distort their meaning.
- Determine if the prophet is foretelling the future. On the other hand, is he simply proclaiming God's

---

[1] Walter A. Elwell and Barry J. Beitzel, *Baker Encyclopedia of the Bible* (Grand Rapids, Mich.: Baker Book House, 1988), 122.

will and purpose to the people. (If prophetic, has any portion of it been fulfilled?)

- The concept of a second fulfillment should be set aside in place of implications.
- Does the New Testament expound on this prophecy?
- The reader needs to slow down and carefully read the account, considering exactly what is being said.
- The Bible student needs to understand the level that the Bible intends to be exact in what is written. If Jim told a friend that 650 graduated with him from high school in 1984, it is not challenged, because it is all too clear that he is using rounded numbers and is not meaning to be exactly precise.
- Unexplained does not equal unexplainable.

Digging into the ancient Jewish mindset, we find that it is dualistic. It views all of God's creation, either on the side of God or Satan. Further, the Jewish mind was determined that regardless of how bad things were, God would come to the rescue of his people. The only pessimistic thinking was their understanding that there had to be a major catastrophe that precipitated the rescue. In combining this way of thinking, they believed that there are two systems of things: (1) the current wicked one that man lives in, and (2) the one that is to come, where God will restore things to the way it was before Adam and Eve sinned. Jehovah impressed upon his people, to see His rescue as imminent. The vision that comes to Daniel in the book of Daniel and John in the book of Revelations, comes in one of two ways: (1) in a dreamed vision state or (2) the person in vision is caught up to heaven and shown what is to take place. Frequently, Isaiah, Daniel and John did not understand the vision; they were simply to pen what they saw. (Isa 6:9-10; 8:16; 29:9-14; 44:18; 53:1; Dan 8:15–26; 9:20–27; 10:18–12:4; Rev 7:13–17; 17:7–18) The people readily recognized the symbolism in most of the prophetic literature, and the less common symbolisms in apocalyptic literature were far more complex, which by design, heighten the desire to interpret and understand them. There are two very important points to keep in mind: (1) some were not meant to be understood fully at the time, and (2) only the righteous ones would have insight into these books, while the wicked would refuse to understand the spiritual things.

Daniel 8:26-27 Updated American Standard Version (UASV)

[26] The vision of the evenings and the mornings that has been told is true,[2] but seal up the vision,[3] for it refers to many days from now."[4]

[27] And I, Daniel, was exhausted and sick for days. Then I got up and carried out the business of the king, and I was disturbed over the vision and no one could understand it.[5]

Daniel 10:14 Updated American Standard Version (UASV)

[14] Now I have come to give you an understanding of what will happen to your people in the end of the days, for it is a vision yet for the days to come."

---

[2] Lit *truth*; Heb., *'emet*

[3] I.e., keep the vision secret; Heb., *satar*

[4] Lit *for to days many*; I.e., to the distant future

[5] Lit *make* me *understand*

Daniel 12:3-4 Updated American Standard Version (UASV)

³ And the ones who are wise will shine brightly like the brightness of the expanse of heaven; and those who turn many to righteousness, like the stars forever and ever. ⁴ But as for you, O Daniel, conceal these words and seal up the book until the time of the end; many will go to and fro,⁶ and knowledge will increase."

Daniel 12:9-10 Updated American Standard Version (UASV)

⁹He said, "Go your way, Daniel, for the words are shut up and sealed until the time of the end. ¹⁰Many shall purify themselves and make themselves white and be refined, but the wicked shall act wickedly. And none of the wicked shall understand, but those who are wise shall understand.

2 Corinthians 4:3-4 Updated American Standard Version (UASV)

³ And even if our gospel is veiled, it is veiled to those who are perishing. ⁴ In their case the god of this world has blinded the minds of the unbelievers, to keep them from seeing the light of the gospel of the glory of Christ, who is the image of God.

One of the principles of interpreting prophecy is to understand judgment prophecies. If a prophet declares judgment on a people, and they turn around from their bad course, the judgment may be lifted, which does not negate the trueness of the prophetic judgment message. There was simply a change in circumstances. There is a principle that most readers are not aware of:

---

⁶ I.e. examine the book thoroughly

Jeremiah 18:7-8 Updated American Standard Version (UASV)

⁷ At one moment I might speak concerning a nation or concerning a kingdom to uproot, to tear down, and to destroy it; ⁸ and if that nation which I have spoken against turns from its evil, I will also feel regret over[7] the calamity that I intended to bring against it.

Another principle that needs to be understood is the language of prophecy. It uses imagery that is common to the people, with the exception of the highly apocalyptic literature. One form of imagery is cosmic.

Isaiah 13:9-11 Updated American Standard Version (UASV)

⁹ Behold, the day of Jehovah is coming,
  cruel, with wrath and burning anger,
to make the land a desolation;
  and he will destroy its sinners from it.
¹⁰ For the stars of the heavens and their constellations
  will not flash forth their light;
the sun will be dark when it rises,
  and the moon will not shed its light.
¹¹ And I will punish the world for its evil,
  and the wicked for their iniquity;
I will put an end to the arrogance of the proud,
  and lay low the haughtiness of tyrants.

It is often assumed that this sort of imagery is talking about the end of the world, and this is not always the case. Using Isaiah 13 as our example, it is talking about a pronouncement against Babylon, not the end of the world, as can be seen in verse 1. This type of terminology is a way of expressing that God is acting on behalf of man. At times, figurative language can come across as

---

[7] Lit *repent of*, .e., *I will change my mind concerning*; or *I will think better of*, or *I will relent concerning*

contradicting for the modern-day reader. For example, in chapter 21 of Revelation the walls of Jerusalem are described as being 200 feet thick. The walls are an image of safety and security for the New Jerusalem. However, in verse 25 we read that the gates are never shut. This immediately leads to the question of why have walls that cannot be penetrated, and then leave the gates open? Moreover, if gates are the weakest point to defend, why have twelve of them (vs. 12)? To the modern militaristic mind, this comes off as contradictory, but not to the Jewish-Christian mind of the first-century. Both present the picture of safety. It is so safe that you can leave the gates open. What about the idea of a "fuller meaning" that the prophet was not aware of? As we saw in the above there would be symbolism meant for a day far into the future, but generally speaking, most prophets proclaimed a message that was applicable to their day and implications for another day. Dr. Robert Stein addresses this issue:

> There are times when a prophetic text appears to have a fulfillment other than what the prophet himself apparently expected. (The following are frequently given as examples: Matt. 1:22–23; 2:15, 17–18; John 12:15; 1 Cor. 10:3–4.) Is it possible that a prophecy may have a deeper meaning or "fuller" sense than the prophet envisioned? . . . Rather than appealing to a "fuller sense" distinct and different from that of the biblical author, however, it may be wiser to see if the supposed sensus plenior is in reality an implication of the author's conscious meaning. Thus, when Paul in 1 Corinthians 9:9 quotes Deuteronomy 25:4 ("do not muzzle an ox while it is treading out the grain") as a justification for ministers of the gospel living off the gospel, this is not a "fuller" meaning of the text unrelated to what the author sought to convey. Rather, it is a legitimate implication of

the willed pattern of meaning contained in Deuteronomy 25:4. If as a principle animals should be allowed to share in the benefits of their work, how much more should the "animal" who is made in the image of God and proclaims the Word of God be allowed to share in the benefits of that work! Thus, what Paul is saying is not a fuller and different meaning from what the writer of Deuteronomy meant. On the contrary, although this specific implication was unknown to him, it is part of his conscious and willed pattern of meaning. Perhaps such prophecies as Matthew 1:22–23 and 2:15 are best understood as revealing implications of the original prophecies in Isaiah 7:14 and Hosea 11:1. Whereas in Isaiah's day the prophet meant that a maiden would give birth to a son who was named "Immanuel," that willed meaning also allows for a virgin one day to give birth to a son who would be Immanuel. Whereas God showed his covenantal faithfulness by leading his "son," his children, back from Egypt to the promised land in Moses' day so also did he lead his "Son," Jesus, back from Egypt to the promised land. [8]

Getting back to Daniel, we can clearly see that his book is prophetic and the only Old Testament apocalyptic book at that, which makes him a special target for the Bible critic. The critic has deemed that Daniel did not pen the book that bears his name, but another writer penned the words some centuries later.[9] These attacks have become

---

[8] Robert H. Stein, *A Basic Guide to Interpreting the Bible: Playing by the Rules* (Grand Rapids, MI: Baker Books, 1994), 97.

[9] Some Bible critics attempt to lessen the charge of forgery by saying that the writer used Daniel as a false name (pseudonym), just as some ancient noncanonical books were written under assumed names. In spite of this, the Bible critic Ferdinand Hitzig held: "The case of the book of Daniel, if it is assigned to any other [writer], is different. Then it becomes

such a reality that most scholars accept the late date of 165 B.C.E., by a pseudonym. As we have learned throughout this book, it is never the majority that establishes something as being true, simply for the fact of being the majority; it is the evidence. If the evidence proves that Daniel did not write the book, then the words are meaningless, and the hope that it contains is not there.

For example, take the allegation made in *The Encyclopedia Americana:* "Many historical details of the earlier periods [such as that of the Babylonian exile] have been badly garbled" in Daniel. Really? We will take up three of those alleged mistakes.

Claims That Belshazzar Is Missing From History

Daniel 5:1, 11, 18, 22, 30 Updated American Standard Version (UASV)

¹ Belshazzar the king made[10] a great feast for a thousand of his nobles, and he was drinking wine in the presence of the thousand.

¹¹ There is a man in your kingdom in whom is a spirit of the holy gods;[11] and in the days of your father, enlightenment, insight and wisdom like the wisdom of the gods were found in him. And King Nebuchadnezzar, your father, your father the king, appointed him chief of the magic-practicing priests, conjurers, Chaldeans and diviners.

¹⁸ You. O king, the Most High God granted the kingdom and the greatness and the glory and the majesty to Nebuchadnezzar your father.

---

a forged writing, and the intention was to deceive his immediate readers, though for their good."

[10] I.e., held

[11] Spirit of ... gods Aram., *ruach-'elahin'*; Or possibly *the Spirit of the holy God*

[22] "But you, his son[12] Belshazzar, have not humbled your heart, although you knew all of this,

[30] That same night Belshazzar the Chaldean king was killed.

In 1850 German scholar Ferdinand Hitzig said in a commentary on the book of Daniel, confidently declaring that Belshazzar was "a figment of the writer's imagination."[13] His reasoning was that Daniel was missing from history, only found in the book of Daniel itself. Does this not seem a bit premature? Is it so irrational to think that a person might not be readily located by archaeology, a brand new field at the time, especially from a period that was yet to be fully explored? Regardless, in 1854, there was a discovery of some small cylinders in the ancient city of Babylon and Ur, southern Iraq. The cuneiform documents were from King Nabonidus, and they included a prayer for "Belshazzar my firstborn son, the offspring of my heart." This discovery was a mere four years after Hitzig made his rash judgment.

Of course, not all critics would be satisfied. H. F. Talbot made the statement, "This proves nothing." The charge by Talbot was that Belshazzar was likely a mere child, but Daniel has him as being king. Well, this critical remark did not even stay alive as long as Hitzig's had. Within the year, more cuneiform tablets were discovered, this time they stated he had secretaries, as well as household staff. Obviously, Belshazzar was not a child! However, more was to come, as other tablets explained that Belshazzar was a coregent king while Nabonidus was away from Babylon for years at a time.[14]

---

[12] Or *descendant*

[13] *Das Buch Daniel*. Ferdinand Hitzig. Weidman (Leipzig) 1850.

[14] When Babylon fell, Nabonidus was away. Therefore, Daniel was correct in that Belshazzar was the king at that time. Critics still try to cling to their Bible difficulty by stating that no secular records state that

One would think that the critic might concede. Still disgruntled, some argued that the Bible calls Belshazzar, the son of Nebuchadnezzar, and not the son of Nabonidus. Others comment that Daniel nowhere mentions the name of Nabonidus. Once again, both arguments are dismantled with a deeper observation. Nabonidus married the daughter of Nebuchadnezzar, making Belshazzar the grandson of Nebuchadnezzar. Both Hebrew and Aramaic language do not have words for "grandfather" or "grandson"; "son of" also means "grandson of" or even "descendant of." (See Matthew 1:1.) Moreover, the account in Daniel does infer that Belshazzar is the son of Nabonidus. When the mysterious handwriting was on the wall, the horrified Belshazzar offered the *third* place in his kingdom, to whoever could interpret it. (Daniel 5:7) The observant reader will notice that Nabonidus held first place in the kingdom, while Daniel held the second place, leaving the third place for the interpreter.

Darius the Mede

One would think that the critic would have learned his lesson from Belshazzar. However, this is just not the case. Daniel 5:31 reads: "and Darius the Mede received the kingdom, being about sixty-two years old." Here again, the critical scholar argues that Darius does not exist, as he has never been found in secular or archaeological records. Therefore, *The New Encyclopædia Britannica* declares that this Darius is "a fictitious character."

There is no doubt that in time; Darius will be unearthed by archaeology, just as Belshazzar has. There is initial information that allows for inferences already. Cuneiform tablets have been discovered that shows Cyrus

---

Belshazzar was a king. When will they quit with this quibbling? Even governors in the Ancient Near East were stated as being kings at times.

the Persian did not take over as the "King of Babylon" directly after the conquest. Rather he carried the title "King of the Lands."[15] W. H Shea suggests, "Whoever bore the title of 'King of Babylon' was a vassal king under Cyrus, not Cyrus himself." Is it possible that Darius is simply a title of a person that was placed in charge of Babylon? Some scholars suggest a man named Gubaru was the real Darius. Secular records do show that Cyrus appointed Gubaru as governor over Babylon, giving him considerable power. Looking to the cuneiform tablets again, we find that Cyrus appointed subgovernors over Babylon. Fascinatingly, Daniel notes that Darius selected 120 satraps to oversee the kingdom of Babylon. – Daniel 6:1.

We should realize that archaeology is continuously bringing unknown people to light all the time, and in time, it may shed more light on Darius. However, for now, and based on the fact that many Bible characters have been established, it is a little ridiculous to consider Darius as "fictitious," worse still to view the whole of the book of Daniel as a fraud. In fact, it is best to see Daniel as a person, who was right there in the midst of that history, giving him access to more court records.

After Belshazzar (King of Babylon), Sargon (Assyrian Monarch), and the like have been assailed with being nonexistent, the Bible critic and liberal scholars do the same with Darius the Mede, and Mordecai in the book of Esther. This illustrates the folly of assigning boundless confidence in the ancient secular records, while we wait in secular sources to validate Scripture. Most outside of true conservative Christianity carries the presupposition that much of the Bible is a myth, legend and erroneous until secular sources support it.

---

[15] This evidence is found in royal titles in economic texts, which just so happens to date to the first two years of Cyrus' rule.

Bible critics argued profusely that Belshazzar was not a historical person. Then, evidence came in that substantiated Belshazzar, and the Bible critic just moves on to another like Sargon, saying that he was not a real historical person, as though they had never raised such an objection for Belshazzar. Then, evidence came in that substantiated Sargon and the Bible critic would silently move on yet again. This is repeated time after time.

The Bible critics, liberal and moderate Bible scholars believe the Bible is wrong until validated by secular history. They move the goal post of trustworthiness as they please so that Scripture will never be authentic and true, it will never be trustworthy, and to these ones, it is not the inspired, fully inerrant Word of God, as far as they are concerned.

Why do we continue to cater to these ones, as though we need to appease them somehow?

King Jehoiakim

Daniel 1:1 Updated American Standard Version (UASV)

¹ In the third year of the reign of Jehoiakim king of Judah, Nebuchadnezzar king of Babylon came to Jerusalem and besieged it.

Jeremiah 25:1 Updated American Standard Version (UASV)

¹ The word that came to Jeremiah concerning all the people of Judah, in the fourth year of Jehoiakim the son of Josiah, king of Judah (that was the first year of Nebuchadnezzar king of Babylon),

Jeremiah 46:2 Updated American Standard Version (UASV)

² About Egypt, concerning the army of Pharaoh Neco king of Egypt, which was by the Euphrates River at Carchemish, which Nebuchadnezzar king of Babylon defeated in the fourth year of Jehoiakim the son of Josiah, king of Judah:

The Bible critic finds fault with Daniel 1:1 as it is not in harmony with Jeremiah, who says "in the fourth year of Jehoiakim the son of Josiah, king of Judah (that was the first year of Nebuchadnezzar king of Babylon)." The Bible student who looks a little deeper will find that there is really no contradiction at all. Pharaoh Necho first made Jehoiakim king in 628 B.C.E. Three years would pass before Nebuchadnezzar succeeded his father as King in Babylon, in 624 B.C.E. In 620 B.C.E., Nebuchadnezzar conquered Judah and made Jehoiakim the subordinate king under Babylon. (2 Kings 23:34; 24:1) Therefore, it is all about the perspective of the writer and where he was when penning his book. Daniel wrote from Babylon; therefore, Jehoiakim's third year would have been when he was made a subordinate king to Babylon. Jeremiah on the other hand wrote from Jerusalem, so he is referring to the time when Jehoiakim was made a subordinate king under Pharaoh Necho.

This so-called discrepancy really just adds more weight to the fact that it was Daniel, who penned the book bearing his name. In addition, it must be remembered that Daniel had Jeremiah's book with him. (Daniel 9:2) Therefore, are we to believe that Daniel was this clever forger, and at the same time, he would contradict the well-known book of Jeremiah, especially in verse 1?

Positive Details

There are many details in the book of Daniel itself, which give credence to its authenticity. For example, Daniel 3:1-6 tells us that Nebuchadnezzar set up a huge image of gold, which his people were to worship. Archaeology has found evidence that credits Nebuchadnezzar with attempts to involve the people more in nationalistic and religious practices. Likewise, Daniel addresses Nebuchadnezzar's arrogant attitude about his many construction plans. (Daniel 4:30) It is not until modern-day archaeology uncovered evidence that we now know Nebuchadnezzar was the person who built much of Babylon. Moreover, his boastful attitude is made quite evident by having his name stamped on the bricks. This fact would not have been something a forger from 167-63 B.C.E. would have known about because the bricks hadn't at that time been unearthed.

The writer of Daniel was very familiar with the differences between Babylonian and Medo-Persian law. The three friends of Daniel were thrown into the fiery furnace for disobeying the Babylonian law, while Daniel, decades later under Persian law, was thrown into a lion's pit for violating the law. (Daniel 3:6; 6:7-9) Archaeology has again proven to be a great help, for they have uncovered an actual letter that shows the fiery furnace was a form of punishment. However, the Medes and Persians would have not used this form of punishment; as fire was sacred to them. Thus, they had other forms of capital punishment.

Another piece of inside knowledge is that Nebuchadnezzar passed and changed laws as he pleased. Darius, on the other hand, was unable to change a law once it was passed, even one that he himself had commissioned. (Daniel 2:5, 6, 24, 46-49; 3:10, 11, 29; 6:12-16) Historian John C. Whitcomb writes: "Ancient history substantiates this difference between Babylon, where the law was subject to the king, and Medo-Persia, where the king was subject to the law."

Daniel 5:1-4 Updated American Standard Version (UASV)

¹ Belshazzar the king made[16] a great feast for a thousand of his nobles, and he was drinking wine in the presence of the thousand.

² Belshazzar, when he tasted the wine, commanded that the vessels of gold and of silver that Nebuchadnezzar his father[17] had taken out of the temple in Jerusalem be brought, that the king and his nobles, his wives, and his concubines might drink from them. ³ Then they brought the gold vessels that had been taken out of the temple, the house of God which was in Jerusalem; and the king and his nobles, his wives and his concubines drank from them. ⁴ They drank the wine and praised the gods of gold and silver, of bronze, iron, wood and stone.

Archaeology has substantiated these kinds of feasts. The fact that stands out is the mention of women being present at the feast, the "wives, and his concubines" were present as well. Such an idea would have been repugnant to the Greeks and Jews of 167-67 B.C.E. era. This may very well be why the Greek Septuagint version of Daniel removed the mention of these women.[18] This so-called forger of Daniel would have live during this same time of the Septuagint.

---

[16] I.e., held

[17] Or *predecessor*; also verses 11, 13, 18

[18] Hebrew scholar C. F. Keil writes of Daniel 5:3: "The LXX. have here, and also at ver. 23, omitted mention of the women, according to the custom of the Macedonians, Greeks, and Romans."

Do External Factors Prove Daniel Is A Forgery?

Even the place of Daniel in the canon of the Hebrew Old Testament is evidence against his having written the book, so says the critics. The Jewish scribes (like Ezra) of ancient Israel arranged the books of the Old Testament into three groups: the Torah, the Prophets, and the Writings. Naturally, we would expect that Daniel would be found among the Prophets, yet they placed him among the Writings. Therefore, the critic makes the argument that Daniel had to of been an unknown when the works of the prophets were being collected. Their theory is that it was placed among the writings because these were collected last.

However, not all Bible scholars agree that the ancient scribes placed Daniel in the Writings, and not the Prophets. However, even if it is as they claim, Daniel was added among the Writings; this does nothing to prove that it was penned at a later date. Old Testament Bible scholar Gleason L. Archer states that . . .

> It should be noted that some of the documents in the Kethubhim [Writings] (the third division of the Hebrew Bible) were of great antiquity, such as the book of Job, the Davidic psalms, and the writings of Solomon. Position in the Kethubhim, therefore, is no proof of a late date of composition. Furthermore the statement in Josephus (Contra Apionem. 1:8) quoted previously in chapter 5 indicates strongly that in the first century A.D., Daniel was included among the prophets in the second division of the Old Testament canon; hence it could not have been assigned to the Kethubim until a later period. 349 The Masoretes may have been influenced in this reassignment by the consideration that Daniel was not appointed or

ordained as a prophet, but remained a civil servant under the prevailing government throughout his entire career. Second, a large percentage of his writings does not bear the character of prophecy, but rather of history (chaps. 1-6), such as does not appear in any of the books of the canonical prophets.350 Little of that which Daniel wrote is couched in the form of a message from God to His people relayed through the mouth of His spokesman. Rather, the predominating element consists of prophetic visions granted personally to the author and interpreted to him by angels.[19]

The critic also turns his attention to the Apocryphal book, Ecclesiasticus, by Jesus Ben Sirach, penned about 180 B.C.E., as evidence that Daniel did not pen the book that bears his name. Ecclesiasticus has a long list of righteous men, of which, Daniel is missing. From this, they conclude that Daniel had to of been an unknown at the time. However, if we follow that line of reasoning; what do we do with the fact that the same list omits: Ezra and Mordecai, good King Jehoshaphat, and the upright man Job; of all the judges, except Samuel.[20] Simply because the above faithful and righteous men are missing from a list in an apocryphal book, are we to dismiss them as having never existed? The very idea is absurd.

---

[19] Archer, Gleason (1996-08-01). A Survey of Old Testament Introduction (Kindle Locations 7963-7972). Moody Publishers.

[20] If we turn our attention to the Apostle Paul's list of faithful men and women found in Hebrews chapter 11; it does appear to mention occasions recorded in Daniel. (Daniel 6:16-24; Hebrews 11:32, 33) Nevertheless, the list by Paul is not an exhaustive list either. Even within his list, Isaiah, Jeremiah, and Ezekiel are not named in the list, but this scarcely demonstrates that they never existed.

Sources in Favor of Daniel

Ezekiel's references to Daniel must be considered to be one of the strongest arguments for a sixth-century date. No satisfactory explanation exists for the use of the name Daniel by the prophet Ezekiel other than that he and Daniel were contemporaries and that Daniel had already become widely known throughout the Babylonian Empire by the time of Ezekiel's ministry.[21]

We have in chapter 9 a series of remarkable predictions which defy any other interpretation but that they point to the coming of Christ and His crucifixion [about] A.D. 30, followed by the destruction of the city of Jerusalem within the ensuing decades. In Dan. 9:25–26, it is stated that sixty-nine heptads of years (i.e., 483 years) will ensue between a "decree" to rebuild the walls of Jerusalem, and the cutting off of Messiah the Prince. In 9:25–26, we read: "Know therefore and understand, that from the going forth of the commandment to restore and to build Jerusalem unto the Messiah the Prince shall be seven weeks, and threescore and two weeks.... And after threescore and two weeks shall Messiah be cut off, but not for himself: and the people of the prince that shall come shall destroy the city and the sanctuary."[22]

---

[21] Stephen R. Miller, vol. 18, *Daniel*, electronic ed., Logos Library System; The New American Commentary (Nashville: Broadman & Holman Publishers, 2001), 42-43.

[22] Gleason Leonard Archer, *A Survey of Old Testament Introduction*, 3rd. ed.]. (Chicago: Moody Press, 1998), 445.

The Greatest Evidence for Daniel

First of all, we have the clear testimony of the Lord Jesus Himself in the Olivet discourse. In Matt. 24:15, He refers to "the abomination of desolation, spoken of through [*dia*] Daniel the prophet." The phrase "abomination of desolation" occurs three times in Daniel (9:27; 11:31; 12:11). If these words of Christ are reliably reported, we can only conclude that He believed the historic Daniel to be the personal author of the prophecies containing this phrase. No other interpretation is possible in the light of the preposition *dia*, which refers to personal agency. It is significant that Jesus regarded this "abomination" as something to be brought to pass in a future age rather than being simply the idol of Zeus set up by Antiochus in the temple, as the Maccabean theorists insist.[23]

While this has certainly been an overview of the evidence in favor of the authenticity of Daniel, there will never be enough to satisfy the critic. One professor at Oxford University wrote: "Nothing is gained by a mere answer to objections, so long as the original prejudice, 'there cannot be supernatural prophecy,' remains." What does this mean? It means that the critic is blinded by his prejudice. However, God has given them the choice of free will.

The Bible critics are ever so vigilant today. They are more prepared than most Christians and witness about their doubts far more than your average Christian witnesses about his or her faith.

---

[23] Gleason Leonard Archer, *A Survey of Old Testament Introduction*, 3rd. ed.]. (Chicago: Moody Press, 1998), 444.

1 Peter 3:15 Updated American Standard Version (UASV)

¹⁵ but sanctify Christ as Lord in your hearts, always being prepared to make a defense[24] to anyone who asks you for a reason for the hope that is in you; yet do it with gentleness and respect;

Peter says that we must be prepared to make a *defense*. The Greek word behind the English "defense" is *apologia* (apologia), which is actually a legal term that refers to the defense of a defendant in court. Our English apologetics is just what Peter spoke of, having the ability to give a reason to any who may challenge us, or to answer those who are not challenging us but who have honest questions that deserve to be answered.

To whom was the apostle Peter talking? Who was Peter saying needed always to be prepared to make a defense? Was he talking only to the pastors, elders, servants, or was he speaking to all Christians? Peter opens this letter saying, "to the chosen who are residing temporarily in the dispersion in Pontus, Galatia, Cappadocia, Asia, and Bithynia." Who are these "chosen" ones? The College Press NIV Commentary gives us the answer,

The Greek text does not include the word "God's," but the translation is a fair one since the clear implication is that God did the choosing. The word Peter uses has a rich biblical heritage. The Jews found their identity and the basis of their lives in the fact that they were God's chosen people (see, e.g., Deut 7:6–8). The New Testament frequently identifies Christians as elect or chosen. In 1 Peter 2:9 Peter will identify Christians as "a chosen people," using the same word ἐκλεκτός (*eklektos*) here translated "elect." The same word is also used of Christ in 2:4 and 6 (where it is translated "chosen"). Christians

---

[24] Or *argument*; or *explanation*

are chosen or elect through the chosen or elect One, Jesus Christ. The idea that Christians are God's chosen people is fundamental to Peter's thinking, as is apparent in 1:13–2:10. Peter is already laying the foundation for his appeals to these Christians to live up to their holy calling. (Black and Black 1998)

The "chosen who are residing temporarily in the dispersion" were Christians, who were living among non-Christian Jews and Gentiles. This letter, then, is addressed to all Christians, but the context of chapters 1:3 to 4:11 is mostly addressed to newly baptized Christians. Therefore, all Christians are obligated to 'be prepared to make a defense to anyone who asks us for a reason for the hope that is in us.' Yes, we are all required to defend our hope successfully. If any have not felt they were up to the task, this author by way of Christian publishing House are publishing books to help along those lines. Here is what is available at present, including this publication you are reading,

THE GREAT TEACHER JESUS CHRIST: What Made Jesus Christ's Teaching, Preaching, Evangelism, and Apologetics Outstandingly Effective? by Edward D. Andrews

THE TEACHER THE APOSTLE PAUL: What Made the Apostle Paul's Teaching, Preaching, Evangelism, and Apologetics Outstanding Effective? by Edward D. Andrews

CHRISTIAN APOLOGETIC EVANGELISM: Reaching Hearts with the Art of Persuasion by Edward D. Andrews

REASONING FROM THE SCRIPTURES: Sharing CHRIST as You Help Others to Learn about the Mighty works of God by Edward D. Andrews

REASONING WITH THE WORLD'S VARIOUS RELIGIONS: Examining and Evangelizing Other Faiths by Edward D. Andrews

CONVERSATIONAL EVANGELISM, [Second Edition] by Edward D. Andrews

THE CHRISTIAN APOLOGIST: Always Being Prepared to Make a Defense [Second Edition] By Edward D. Andrews

CHRISTIAN APOLOGETIC EVANGELISM: Reaching Hearts with the Art of Persuasion by Edward D Andrews

THE EVANGELISM HANDBOOK: How All Christians Can Effectively Share God's Word in Their Community, [SECOND EDITION], by Edward D. Andrews

These first-century Christians in Asia Minor were in a time of difficulty. They were at the time of Peter's letter; about 62-64 C.E. going through some trials, not knowing that many far more severe lie in the not too distant future. Within a few years, the persecution of Christians by Emperor Nero would begin. These new converts had given up former religions, idols, cults and superstitions, their 'the futile ways inherited from your forefathers.' (1 Pet. 1:18) These ones were taking off their old person, and bringing their lives in harmony with God's Word, such as 'malice and deceit and hypocrisy and envy and slander.' (1 Pet. 2:1) Now they were 'no longer living for the lusts of men, but for the will of God.' (1 Pet. 4:2) Their former pagan friends now hated these new Christians, because 'they were surprised when these chosen ones do not join them in the same flood of debauchery, and they maligned them.' (1 Pet. 4:4) In fact, Peter informs us that Satan, the Devil is enraged when one is converted from their former life of debauchery, conformed instead to the Word of God. Peter warned them, "Be sober-minded; be watchful. Your adversary the devil prowls around like a roaring lion, seeking someone to devour." 1 Peter 5:8

Christians have never really had it easy in defending their hope. Peter counsels these new ones, who have next to no experience in coping with trials and persecutions to rejoice, albeit distressed by numerous trials. "**Keep your conduct among the Gentiles honorable**, so that when they speak against you as evildoers, they may see your good deeds and glorify God on the day of visitation." (1 Pet. 2:12) "The end of all things is at hand; therefore **be self-controlled and sober-minded for the sake of your prayers**." 1 Pet. 4:4) "Be sober-minded; be watchful" in the midst of men who continue "living in sensuality, passions, drunkenness, orgies, drinking parties, and lawless idolatry." (1 Pet. 4:3) They should be united under Christ as they 'Have purified their souls by their obedience to the truth for a sincere brotherly love, love one another earnestly from a pure heart." (1 Peter 1:22) "Above all, [they were to] keep loving one another earnestly, since love covers a multitude of sins. Show hospitality to one another without grumbling. As each has received a gift, use it to serve one another, as good stewards of God's varied grace." (1 Pet 4:8-10) 'Finally, all of them, had unity of mind, sympathy, brotherly love, a tender heart, and a humble mind. They did not repay evil for evil or reviling for reviling, but on the contrary, they blessed, for to this they were called, that you may obtain a blessing.' (1 Pet. 3:8-9) If they heeded this counsel, it would have kept them from falling or drifting back into their former ways.

There was one more obligation if they were to preserve on the right path of conduct, namely, being prepared to make a defense for their hope. "It was revealed to [the prophets] that they were serving not themselves but you, in the things that have now been announced to you through those who preached the good news to you by the Holy Spirit sent from heaven, things into which angels long to look. Therefore, preparing your minds for action, and being sober-minded, set your hope fully on the grace that will be brought to you at the revelation of Jesus Christ." (1 Pet. 1:12-13) Peter went on to tell them that they were "a chosen race, a royal priesthood, a holy nation, a people for his own possession, that you may proclaim the excellencies of him who called you out of darkness into his marvelous light." (1 Pet. 2:9) When should they "proclaim these excellencies"? He writes, "but in your hearts honor Christ the Lord as holy, **always being prepared** to make a defense to anyone who asks you for a reason for the hope that is in you; yet do it with gentleness and respect." 1 Peter 3:15

The world in which we live today is much more vast than that of the first-century up unto the 21st-century. The trials and persecution today are much more intense, which unfortunately we ca watch around the world, by way of the media and social media. The greatest threat to Christianity is Islam, which has been an ardent enemy of Christianity since the seventh-century C.E. They are slaughtering Christians the world over. They view Christians as the big Satan and the Jews as little Satan. In their theology, they are looking to turn the world into one big Islamic state, governed by the Quran. For the more radical aspects of Islam, it is convert to Islam or be killed as an infidel.

Recommended Reading

THE GUIDE TO ANSWERING ISLAM: What Every Christian Needs to Know About Islam and the Rise of Radical Islam by Daniel Janosik

UNDERSTANDING ISLAM AND TERRORISM: A Biblical Point of View by Kerby Anderson

IS THE QURAN THE WORD OF GOD?: Is Islam the One True Faith? By Edward D. Andrews

The second greatest threat to tradition and conservatism is liberal Christianity. Their continued dissecting of the Scriptures until Moses did not pen the first five books, Isaiah is not the author of the book that bears his name, nor is Daniel the author of the book that bears his name, and the Bible is full of myths and legends, errors and contractions.

Then, as we have seen throughout this publication, there are moderate and liberal Bible scholars, who are advocates of Historical Criticism Methodology, and its sub-criticisms: Source Criticism, Tradition Criticism, Form Criticism, Redaction Criticism, among others.

2 Timothy 2:24-25 Updated American Standard Version (ASV)

[24] For a slave of the Lord does not need to fight, but needs to be kind to all, qualified to teach, showing restraint when wronged, [25] instructing his opponents with gentleness, if perhaps God may grant them repentance leading to accurate knowledge [*epignosis*][25] of the truth,

Look at the Greek word (*epignosis*) behind the English "knowledge" from above. "It is more intensive than *gnosis* (knowledge) because it expresses a more thorough participation in the acquiring of knowledge on the part of the learner."[26] The requirement of all of the Lord's servants is that they be able to teach, but not in a quarrelsome way, but in a way to correct opponents with mildness. Why? The purpose of it all is that by God, yet through the Christian teacher, one may come to repentance and begin taking in accurate knowledge of the truth.

> Some Christians see apologetics as pre-evangelism; it is not the gospel, but it prepares the soil for the gospel.[27] Others make no such

---

[25] *Epignosis* is a strengthened or intensified form of *gnosis* (*epi*, meaning "additional"), meaning, "true," "real," "full," "complete" or "accurate," depending upon the context. Paul and Peter alone use *epignosis*.

26. Spiros Zodhiates, *The Complete Word Study Dictionary: New Testament*, Electronic ed. (Chattanooga, TN: AMG Publishers, 2000, c1992, c1993), S. G1922.

[27] Norman Geisler and Ron Brooks, When Skeptics Ask (Grand Rapids: Baker Books, 1996), 11.

distinction, seeing apologetics, theology, philosophy, and evangelism as deeply entwined facets of the gospel.[28] Whatever its relation to the gospel, apologetics **is an extremely important enterprise that can profoundly impact unbelievers** and be used as the tool that clears the way to faith in Jesus Christ. (Bold mine.)

Many Christians did not come to believe as a result of investigating the Bible's authority, the evidence for the resurrection, or as a response to the philosophical arguments for God's existence. They responded to the proclamation of the gospel. Although these people have reasons for their belief, they are deeply personal reasons that often do not make sense to unbelievers. **They know the truth but are not necessarily equipped to share or articulate the truth in a way that is understandable** to those who have questions about their faith. It is quite possible to believe something is true without having a proper understanding of it or the ability to articulate it. (Bold mine.)

Christians who believe but do not know why are often insecure and comfortable only around other Christians. Defensiveness can quickly surface when challenges arise on issues of faith, morality, and truth because of a lack of information regarding the rational grounds for Christianity. At its worst, this can lead to either a fortress mentality or a belligerent faith, precisely the opposite of the Great Commission Jesus gave in Matthew 28:19–20. The Christian's charge is not to withdraw from the world and

---

[28] Greg Bahnsen, Van Til Apologetic (Phillipsburg, NJ: Presbyterian and Reformed, 1998), 43.

lead an insular life. Rather, we must be engaged in the culture, to be salt and light.

The solution to this problem requires believers to become informed in doctrine, the history of their faith, philosophy, logic, and other disciplines as they relate to Christianity. Believers must know the facts, arguments and theology and understand how to employ them in a way that will effectively engage the culture. Believers need Christian apologetics. One of the first tasks of Christian apologetics provides information. A number of widely held assumptions about Christianity can be easily challenged with a little information. This is even true for persons who are generally well-educated.[29]

The ability to reason with others will take time, practice and patience. For example, if someone reasons with others successfully, that person must be reasonable. In a discussion about the historicity about Jesus, a believer knows the other person denying the existence of Jesus is wrong. Moreover, believers possess a truckload of evidence to support this position. However, it is best sometimes to not unload the truck by dumping the entire load at a listener's feet in one conversation, or in one breath. Being reasonable does not mean that a believer compromises the truth because he or she does not unload on the listener.

The other person will likely make many wrong statements in the conversation, and we should let most of them go unchallenged; rather, focus on a handful of the most crucial pieces of evidence and do not get lost by refuting every wrong statement. He may make bold

---

[29] Powell, Doug (2006-07-01). *Holman QuickSource Guide to Christian Apologetics* (Holman Quicksource Guides) (p. 6-7). B&H Publishing. Kindle Edition.

condemnatory statements about many Christian beliefs, but we need to remain calm and not make a big deal of those statements. Listen carefully to the other person, and stay within the boundaries of the evidence in the conversation. For example, in a conversation on the historicity of Jesus when the listener states, "The New Testament manuscripts were completely corrupted in the copying process for a millennium, to the point that we do not even have the supposed Word of God." The evidence for the historicity of Jesus rests in the first and second century, so it would be a fool's errand to get into an extensive side subject about the restoration of the New Testament text, which took place over the centuries that followed the first two centuries C.E. There will be another day to talk about the history of the Greek New Testament, but today focus on the historicity of Jesus Christ.

God has given humanity free will, meaning each human has the right to choose, even if that choice is unwise. Believers have the assignment of proclaiming "the good news of the kingdom," as well as "making disciples" of redeemable humankind. Therefore, we must not pressure, coerce, or force people to accept the truth of that "Good News." However, all Christians have an obligation to reason with anyone by respectfully, gently, and mildly overturning their false reasoning, in the attempt that being used by God we may save some.

Evidence that Revelation Is Authentic and Inspired

1 Revelation of Jesus Christ which gave to him
Ἀποκάλυψις Ἰησοῦ , ἣν ἔδωκεν αὐτῷ
the God to show to the slaves of him
ὁ θεὸς δεῖξαι τοῖς δούλοις αὐτοῦ,
which (things it is binding to occur in quickness and
ἃ δεῖ γενέσθαι ἐν , καὶ

he showed by signs having sent off through the   angel
ἐσήμανεν   ἀποστείλας   διὰ   τοῦ ἀγγέλου
of him to the   slave   of him
αὐτοῦ τῷ δούλῳ αὐτοῦ Ἰωάνει,

1 Ἀποκάλυψις Ἰησοῦ Χριστοῦ ἣν ἔδωκεν αὐτῷ ὁ θεὸς
Revelation of Jesus   Christ   that   gave   to him the God

δεῖξαι τοῖς δούλοις αὐτοῦ   ἃ   δεῖ   γενέσθαι ἐν τάχει ,
to show to the slaves of him what is necessary to become in quickness

καὶ ἐσήμανεν   ἀποστείλας   διὰ τοῦ ἀγγέλου αὐτοῦ τῷ
and he signified having delegated through the messenger of him to the

δούλῳ αὐτοῦ Ἰωάννῃ,
slave of him **John**
30

Revelation 1:1 Updated American Standard Version (UASV)

1 The revelation of Jesus Christ, which God gave him, to show his slaves the things that must shortly take place; and he sent his angel and presented it in signs through him to his slave **John,**

Who is John that is referred to as the author of Revelation? The account above from 1:1 tells us that he was a slave of Jesus Christ and 1:9 tells us, "I John, **your brother** and a **sharer with you in the tribulation** and kingdom and the patient endurance that are in Jesus, was **on the island called Patmos** because of the word of God and the testimony about Jesus." This being so vague means that the author must have been well-known to his readers as no further identification was necessary. The most well-known John was the apostle John. Papias, who wrote in the first part of the second century C.E., is said to have held the book to be of apostolic origin. Says Justin Martyr,

---

[30]Eberhard Nestle et al., *The Greek New Testament*, 27th ed. (Deutsche Bibelgesellschaft: Stuttgart, 1993), Re 1.

of the second century, "There was a certain man with us, whose name was John, one of the apostles of Christ, who prophesied, by a revelation that was made to him."[31]

Some have argued that the apostle John's other writings contained a tremendous emphasis on love, which they use to suggest that he could have written Revelation. However, a different genre of writing called for a very forceful and dynamic writing style. If we recall it was John and his brother James, who was filled with indignation against the Samaritans of a certain city, to the point where they wanted to call down fire from heaven. That is why they were given the surname "Boanerges, that is, "Sons of Thunder" (Mark 3:17; Luke 9:54) Again, this departure in writing style should cause no difficulty when we remember that in Revelation the subject matter has changed. What John was shown in these visions is unlike anything he had ever seen before. Moreover, it is the Holy Spirit that gave him his subject matter. In addition, we must keep in mind the extraordinary harmony of the book with the rest of the prophetic Scriptures indisputably proves it to be an authentic, fully inerrant part of the inspired Word of God.[32] Lastly, Dr. Norman L. Geisler writes,

---

[31] Justin Martyr *Dialogue with Trypho* 81, in *The Ante-Nicene Fathers*, ed. Alexander Roberts and James Donaldson, vol. 1, *The Apostolic Fathers, Justin Martyr, and Irenaeus* (reprint, Grand Rapids: Eerdmans, n.d.), p. 240. Note that the elapsed time between John's death (presumably in a.d. 98) and Justin Martyr's comment is less then forty years, when eyewitnesses could still testify to the veracity of his statement. Irenaeus (Eusebius *Eccl. Hist.* 3.39.5–6) writes that the apostle John lived "until the times of Trajan," who was emperor from 98 to 117.

[32] Geisler writes, "External Evidence (1) Justin Martyr called the author 'A certain man among us, whose name was John, one of the apostles of Christ …' (Justin, Against Heresies). (2) Irenaeus, an early resident of Asia, cited it as John's writing. (3) The Shepherd of Hernias refers to it. (4) The early Muratorian canon includes it in the Bible. (5) Other early Fathers cited it as coming from John the apostle, including Tertullian, Hippolytus, Clement of Alexandria, Origen, Athanasius, and Augustine. (6) Later voices to reject John's authorship did so on dogmatic grounds, largely because they opposed John's millennialism (chap. 20)

No one else but the apostle John could use just his name, John, and have his book accepted. (3) It is the only book, other than the Gospel of John (also written by the apostle John), to refer to Christ as the Word (Logos) in the personal sense (John 1:1; Rev. 19:13). (4) The basic style and content use of the Greek fit the apostle John.' (5) The vocabulary has a strong overlap, with 416 words in the Gospel the same as 913 separate words in Revelation. (6) The author's detailed knowledge of the land and events fits the apostle John (chaps. 1-3).[33]

When we look at the earliest evidence, the late date of 95 C.E. fits the apostle John alone, as he lived to 100 C.E., which was twenty-five years after the destruction of Jerusalem. This would have been toward the end of the reign of Emperor Domitian (81-96 C.E.). In verification of this, Irenaeus (born between 120 C.E. and 140 C.E.; died about 200 C.E.) in his "Against Heresies" says of the Apocalypse, "For that was seen no very long time since, but almost in our day, towards the end of Domitian's reign.[34] both Eusebius and Jerome agree with this testimony.

Roman Emperor Titus (79-81 C.E.) was the brother of Domitian. It was then general Titus, who formerly had directed the effective assault on Jerusalem, destroying the

---

and used an allegorical method of interpretation. (7) The alleged assertion by Papias that John was martyred before AU) 70 is contradicted by many other sources (see points 1-6) and is subject to other interpretations." – Norman Geisler. *A Popular Survey of the New Testament*, (pp. 310-311).

[33] Norman Geisler. *A Popular Survey of the New Testament*, (p. 310).

[34] Irenaeus of Lyons, "Irenæus against Heresies," in *The Apostolic Fathers with Justin Martyr and Irenaeus*, ed. Alexander Roberts, James Donaldson, and A. Cleveland Coxe, vol. 1, The Ante-Nicene Fathers (Buffalo, NY: Christian Literature Company, 1885), 559–560.

city. Domitian became the emperor at the death of Titus, fifteen years before the book of Revelation was penned. He commanded that he be worshiped as god and took the title "*Dominus et Deus noster ('our Lord and God')*."[35] The first-century Christian could not and would not in worship of false gods, as they refused to compromise their faith. It was at the end of Domitian's reign when extremely severe persecution was being handed out to the Christians that John was exiled to Patmos by Domitian. It was in 96 C.E. that Domitian was assassinated, wherein he was succeeded by the more tolerant emperor Nerva, who was the one to release John from Patmos. John wrote down these visions that he saw while he was imprisoned on Patmos.

---

[35] Grant R. Osborne, *Revelation*, Baker Exegetical Commentary on the New Testament (Grand Rapids, MI: Baker Academic, 2002), 513.

CHAPTER 2 Interpreting Prophecy

Most understand the word "prophecy" to be another word for prediction. The Hebrew, *navi* and the Greek *prophētēs* (prophet), carry the meaning of one who is a proclaimer of God's message and need not necessarily be foretelling of the future. He may very well be proclaiming a moral teaching, an expression of a divine command or judgment, but they also mean a foretelling of something to come. Below, we will be considering the secondary meaning of prophecy, one who for *foretells* the future, not the primary meaning, one who *forth tells* the will and purpose of God, i.e. a proclaimer. Just as it is true of all these genres, there are principles that both writer and reader were aware of, and need be explained. We, however, are far removed from their time and need to be introduced to these principles.

The Prophetic Judgment of Nineveh

Deuteronomy 18:20-22 Updated American standard Version (UASV)

20 But the prophet who speaks a word presumptuously in my name which I have not commanded him to speak, or which he speaks in the name of other gods, that prophet shall die.' 21 You may say in your heart, 'How will we know the word which Jehovah has not spoken?' 22 When a prophet speaks in the name of Jehovah, if the word does not come to pass or come true, that is a word that Jehovah has not spoken; the prophet has spoken it presumptuously; you shall not be afraid of him.

Jonah 3:4-5 Updated American standard Version (UASV)

⁴ And Jonah began to go into the city a journey of one day, and he cried out and said, "Yet forty days, and Nineveh shall be overthrown!" ⁵ And the people of Nineveh believed God. They called for a fast and put on sackcloth, from the greatest of them to the least of them.

Jonah 3:10 Updated American standard Version (UASV)

¹⁰ When God saw their deeds, that they turned from their wicked way, then God relented concerning the calamity which he had said he would do to them, and he did not do it.

Based on Deuteronomy 18:20-222, does Jonah 3:4-5 and 10 not prove that Jonah was a false prophet. No, both Jonah and the Ninevites were aware of a principle that is often overlooked by the modern-day reader. Both Jeremiah and Ezekiel give the answer or the principle that readers of that time would have understood about judgment prophecy. Jeremiah explicitly explains the rule of judgment prophecies, when he writes,

Jeremiah 18:7-8 Updated American standard Version (UASV)

⁷ At one moment I might speak concerning a nation or concerning a kingdom to uproot, to tear down, and to destroy it; ⁸ and if that nation which I have spoken against turns from its evil, I will also feel regret over[36] the calamity that I intended to bring against it.

The opposite is true as well,

---

[36] Lit *repent of*; .e., *I will change my mind concerning*; or *I will think better of*, or *I will relent concerning*

Jeremiah 18:9-10 Updated American standard Version (UASV)

⁹ Or at another moment I might speak concerning a nation or concerning a kingdom to build up or to plant it; ¹⁰ if it does evil in my eyes by not obeying my voice, then I will feel regret over[37] the good with which I had promised to bless it.

Yes, if one turns back from their evil ways, endeavoring to obey God's Word, he will not receive the condemnatory judgment that he deserves. That a previous wicked deed will not be held against them, God states,

Ezekiel 33:13-16 Updated American standard Version (UASV)

¹³ When I say to the righteous one: "You will surely keep living," and he trusts in his own righteousness and does injustice, none of his righteous acts will be remembered, but he will die for the wrong that he has done. ¹⁴ "'And when I say to the wicked one: "You will surely die," and he turns away from his sin and does what is just and righteous, ¹⁵ and the wicked one returns what was taken in pledge and pays back what was taken by robbery, and he walks in the statutes of life by not doing what is wrong, he will surely keep living. He will not die. ¹⁶ None of his sins that he has committed will be remembered against him. He has practiced justice and righteousness; he shall surely live.

Regardless of all that one has done throughout their life, it is their standing in God's eyes at the time of the divine judgment, which God considers. Therefore, God goes on to say through Ezekiel, "None of his sins that he has committed will be remembered against him."

---

[37] Lit *repent*; I.e., *I will change my mind concerning*; or *I will think better of*, or *I will relent concerning*

Supposed Unfulfilled Prophecy

In the days when Micah was prophesying, c. 777-717, the king, the heads of the Jerusalem government, the religious leaders, the priests, and some prophets, were deserving of nothing but death. All were guilty of causing the life of their fellow countrymen, all for the sake of greed. They were guilty of false worship, bribery, lies, and wicked behavior. These leaders used false prophets, who were not true spokesmen of God. Therefore, the real prophet, Micah, shouted,

Micah 3:12 Updated American Standard Version (UASV)

[12] Therefore because of you
   Zion shall be plowed as a field;
Jerusalem shall become a heap of ruins,
   and the mountain[38] of the house as a high place in a forest.

The destruction occurred in the late seventh-century B.C.E., just as it was prophesied. As we can see below, Micah 3:12 was quoted over a century later in Jeremiah 26:18.

Jeremiah 26:16-19 Updated American Standard Version (UASV)

[16] Then the officials and all the people said to the priests and the prophets, "This man is not worthy of death; for he hath spoken to us in the name of Jehovah our God." [17] Then rose up certain of the elders of the land, and spoke to all the assembly of the people, saying, [18] "Micah the Morashtite prophesied in the days of Hezekiah king of

---

[38] I.e., *the temple mount*

Judah; and he spoke to all the people of Judah, saying: 'Thus says Jehovah of hosts,

"'Zion shall be plowed as a field;
Jerusalem shall become a heap of ruins,
and the mountain of the house a wooded height.'

[19] Did Hezekiah king of Judah and all Judah put him to death? Did he not fear Jehovah and entreat the favor of Jehovah, and Jehovah changed his mind about the misfortune, which he had pronounced against them? But we are committing a great evil against our own souls."

Is this another unfulfilled prophecy? Did not Jeremiah himself say, "Jehovah changed his mind about the misfortune, which he had pronounced against them"? Verse 19 of Jeremiah [chapter 26] "indicates that Micah's preaching may have been instrumental in the revival under King Hezekiah (see 2 Kgs 18:1–6; 2 Chr 29–31)." (Barker and Bailey 2001, 82) The New American Commentary authors go on to say,

> Lamentations describes the awful fulfillment of this prophecy (see Introduction, p. 30).[39] It is ironic that those who thought they were the builders of Zion (v. 10) actually turned out to be, in a sense, its destroyers. The Lord, because of their breach of covenant, used King Nebuchadnezzar's Neo-Babylonian army to raze Jerusalem and its temple. They were reduced to a "mound of ruins" (translating the Hb. word *'îyyîn*) similar to an archaeological tell and to Ai (see also comments on 1:6), foreshadowing the Roman destruction of a.d. 70. Jerusalem became a place suitable only for wild animals. And the temple mount that thronged with worshipers became as deserted as

---

[39] Cf. Lam 1:1, 4, 6, 18–19; 2:2, 6, 9–10, 20; 5:17–18, etc.

when Abraham almost offered Isaac there on Mount Moriah (Gen 22:2, 14). (Barker and Bailey 2001, 82)

Yes, there is no reason to view Micah's words as an unfulfilled prophecy. What we have here is a following of the above rule, with a qualifying clause, so to speak. As God said through Jeremiah, "If at any time I say that I am going to uproot, break down, or destroy any nation or kingdom, but then that nation turns from its evil, I will not do what I said I would." (17:7-8) However, "if I say that I am going to plant or build up any nation or kingdom, but then that nation disobeys me and does evil, I will not do what I said I would." In other words, the king, the governmental leaders, and the priests heeded Micah's warning, repented, and were forgiven for a time, with the judgment prophecy lifted. However, they fell back into their former ways, even more grievously than before. Therefore, Micah's prophecy was reinstated. It is as Jeremiah said in 26:19, "But we are committing a great evil against our own souls." Therefore, Jeremiah was saying, Micah prophesied, the people repented, God forgave them, and now Micah's words will be carried out, because of the current generation of God's people 'committing a great evil against their own souls.'

As we can see from the above, judgment prophecies are based on a continued wrong course by those receiving condemnation. However, both the condemned and the one proclaiming the prophecy knew that the judgment would be lifted if they reversed course, and repented. This was even expressed by Jonah himself. "But it displeased Jonah exceedingly, and he was angry. And he prayed to Jehovah and said, "O Jehovah, is not this what I said when I was yet in my country? That is why I made haste to flee to Tarshish; for I knew that you are a gracious God and merciful, slow to anger and abounding in steadfast love, and relenting from disaster." (4:1-2) However, it is also true, if one goes in the opposite direction after having repented, returning to the sinful ways, the judgment will be reinstated.

Prophetic Language

The prophet is much like the poet, in that he is given a license to express himself in nonliteral language. Generally, he is working with images that are far more effective than words themselves.

Matthew 24:29-31 Updated American Standard Version (UASV)

The Coming of the Son of Man

[29] "But immediately after the tribulation of those days the sun will be darkened, and the moon will not give its light, and the stars will fall from heaven, and the powers of the heavens will be shaken. [30] And then will appear in heaven the sign of the Son of Man, and then all the tribes of the earth will mourn, and they will see the Son of Man coming on the clouds of heaven with power and great glory. [31] And he will send forth his angels with a great trumpet call, and they will gather his chosen ones from the four winds, from one end of heaven to the other.

The above cosmic terminology need not be taken literally. It is a part of their toolkit, which enables them to make it clear that God is acting on behalf of humans. (See Dan. 2:21; 4:17, 25, 34–35; 5:21) The sun is not going to be darkened, the moon will not stop giving its light, the stars are not going to fall from the heavens, nor will the heavens be shaken. What is being communicated here is that following the tribulation when God is going to judge humans, the righteous will receive life, and the unrighteous will cut off from life. (34-45) While we do not take cosmic terminology literally, we do discover its meaning, and this is what we are to take literally.

Acts 2:14-21 Updated American Standard Version (UASV)

Peter's Sermon at Pentecost

¹⁴ But Peter, standing with the eleven, lifted up his voice and declared to them, "Men of Judea and all who dwell in Jerusalem, let this be known to you, and give ear to my words. ¹⁵ For these men are not drunk, as you suppose, since it is only the third hour of the day;[40] ¹⁶ but this is what was spoken of through the prophet Joel

¹⁷ "'And it shall be in the last days, God says,
that I will pour out my Spirit on all flesh,
and your sons and your daughters shall prophesy,
 and your young men shall see visions,
 and your old men shall dream dreams;
¹⁸ and even on my male slaves and on my female slaves
 I will pour out some of my Spirit in those days, and they will prophesy.
¹⁹ And I will show wonders in the heavens above
 and signs on the earth below,
 blood, and fire, and vapor of smoke;
²⁰ the sun shall be turned to darkness
 and the moon to blood,
 before the great and glorious day of the Lord comes.
²¹ And it shall come to pass that everyone who calls upon the name of the Lord will be saved.'[41]

In all occurrences, prophecy proclaimed in Bible times had meaning to the people who heard it; it served for their guidance as well as each generation up unto the time of its fulfillment. Usually, it had some fulfillment in that time, in numerous instances being fulfilled during the days of that very generation. In looking at Peters quote from Joel, it must be asked; did they see those cosmic events on

---

[40] I.e. 9 a.m.

[41] A quotation from Joel 2:28-32

Pentecost? Yes, the cosmic terminology is expressing that God was acting on behalf of those first Christians. A new era was being entered, and God did pour out His Spirit, and sons and daughters did prophesy, both in proclaiming a message and in the foretelling of further events. However, let us delve even deeper into prophecy and how they are to be interpreted. Before moving on, let us briefly offer what we have learned thus far:

- Judgment prophecies could be lifted, set aside if the parties affected repent and turnaround from their former course.

- On the other hand, if God has promised blessings but then that person or group disobeys him and does evil, he will not do what he had said he would do.

- Then again, if one has repented, turned around, and a judgment prophecy has been lifted, it can be reinstated if that person or group return to their former evil ways.

- Prophets have a license to use prophetic language, cosmic terminology that evidences that God is working or acting within humanity.

- While we do not take cosmic terminology literally, we do discover its meaning, and this is what we are to take literally.

Interpreting Prophecy

If we are to understand and interpret prophecy correctly, we must first have a grasp of the figurative language, types, and symbols. We have already dealt with figurative language back in the CHRISTIAN PUBLISHING

HOUSE BLOG Interpreting Figurative Language,[42] and typology is dealt with throughout this book. In addition, the reader should carefully consider New Testament Writers Use of the Old Testament.[43]

We will follow the same interpretation process here that we would elsewhere, grammatical-historical interpretation, which attempts to ascertain what the author meant by the words that he used, which should have been understood by his original readers. (Stein 1994, 38-9) It was the primary method of interpretation when higher criticism's Historical-Critical Method was in its infancy back in the 19th century (Milton Terry), and remains the only method of interpretation for true conservative scholarship in the later 20th century into the 21st century.

Grammatical Aspect

When we speak of interpreting the Bible grammatically, we are referring to the process of seeking to determine its meaning by ascertaining four things: (a) the meaning of words (lexicology), (b) the form of words (morphology), (c) the function of words (parts of speech), and (d) the relationships of words (syntax). In the meaning of words (lexicology), we are concerned with (a) etymology- how words are derived and developed, (b) usage how words are used by the same and other authors, (c) synonyms and antonyms -how similar and opposite words are used, and (d) context-how words are used in various contexts.

---

[42] https://christianpublishinghouse.co/2016/10/28/interpreting-figurative-language/

[43] https://christianpublishinghouse.co/2016/12/07/interpreting-new-testament-writers-use-of-the-old-testament/

In discussing the form of words (morphology), we are looking at how words are structured and how that affects their meaning. For example, the word eat means something different from ate, though the same letters are used. The word part changes meaning when the letter "s" is added to it to make the word parts. The function of words (parts of speech) considers what the various forms do. These include attention to subjects, verbs, objects, nouns, and others, as will be discussed later. The relationships of words (syntax) are the way words are related or put together to form phrases, clauses, and sentences. (Zuck 1991, 100-101)

Historical Aspect

By "historical" we mean the setting in which the prophet's book was written and the circumstances involved in the writing. ... taking into consideration the circumstances of the writings and the cultural environment. We must keep in mind that even though many of the prophetic utterances were meant for the generation, in which they were spoken, or shortly thereafter. Even if it is not the immediate generation, all prophetic utterances had some type of meaning to the prophet's generation, be it hope in some future person or event, or the knowledge of a judgment that is coming or could come as a result of their behavior. For example, maybe the Israelites are under persecution and oppression by the surrounding nations, and the prophecy is for a protector that is to rise up, and set matters straight. Even though they do not know, who the protector is, or the exact time of his appearance, they do know that God cannot lie, nor has he ever lied, and so, they can have hope and faith in his words. Moreover, they would have also known that if they fell back into false worship, God could withdraw his prophetic message of a savior.

The context in which a given Scripture passage is written influences how that passage is to be understood. Context includes several things:

- the verse(s) immediately before and after a passage
- the paragraph and book in which the verses occur
- the dispensation in which it was written
- the message of the entire Bible
- the historical-cultural environment of that time when it was written. (Zuck 1991, 77)

What are the last days, when did they start, and how long are they to run? The Bible says that "the last days" would be "difficult times will come." Does that description match the period in which we now live?

In Bible prophecy, "**Last Days**. Expression used in Scripture to describe the final period of the world as we now know it. In the OT the last days are anticipated as the age of messianic fulfillment (see Is 2:2; Mi 4:1), and the NT writers regard themselves as living in the last days, the era of the gospel. Thus, for example, Peter explains that the events of the day of Pentecost are the fulfillment of Joel 2:28: "This is what was spoken by the prophet Joel: 'And in the last days it shall be, God declares, that I will pour out my Spirit upon all flesh' " (Acts 2:16, 17); and the author of the letter to the Hebrews declares that God "spoke of old to our fathers by the prophets; but in these last days has spoken to us by a Son" (Heb 1:1). The last days, then, are the days of evangelical blessing in which the benefits of the salvation procured by the perfect life, death, resurrection, and glorification of Jesus Christ are freely available throughout the world. They are the days of opportunity for unbelievers to repent and turn to God, and of responsibility for believers to proclaim the gospel message throughout the world."[44]

Difficult Times in the Last Days

2 Timothy 3:1-7 Updated American Standard Version (UASV)

3 But realize this, that **in the last days difficult times will come.** [2] For men will be lovers of themselves, lovers of money, boastful, arrogant, revilers, disobedient to parents, ungrateful, unholy, [3] unloving, irreconcilable, malicious gossips, without self-control, brutal, not loving good, [4] treacherous, reckless, conceited, lovers of pleasure rather than lovers of God, [5] having the appearance of godliness, but denying its power; avoid such men as these. [6] For among them are those who enter into households and captivate weak women weighed down with sins, led on by various desires, [7] always learning and yet never able to come to an accurate knowledge[45] of truth.

On this Knute Larson writes, "The 'last days' is not some future event to which we look. It is now. Jesus Christ initiated this epoch, and it will continue uninterrupted until his return. Paul defined this expansive time period as "terrible." God's extravagant grace also characterizes this era, establishing salvation and the church. But these days unleash Satan's wild attempts to destroy and undermine God's redemptive intentions. In giving us this information, Paul desired that believers maintain a readiness of spirit and life. The battle will rage. What each believer must

---

[44] Walter A. Elwell and Barry J. Beitzel, "Last Days," *Baker Encyclopedia of the Bible* (Grand Rapids, MI: Baker Book House, 1988), 1310.

[45] *Epignosis* is a strengthened or intensified form of *gnosis* (*epi*, meaning "additional"), meaning, "true," "real," "full," "complete" or "accurate," depending upon the context. Paul and Peter alone use *epignosis*.

decide is whether he will prepare for the promised difficulties or given to personal safety and comfort.[46]

---

[46] Knute Larson, *I & II Thessalonians, I & II Timothy, Titus, Philemon*, vol. 9, Holman New Testament Commentary (Nashville, TN: Broadman & Holman Publishers, 2000), 300.

CHAPTER 3 The Kings of the South and the North

Daniel 11:1-9 (530 – 226 B.C.E.)

Daniel 8:17, 19, 26 Updated American Standard Version (UASV)

17 So he came near where I stood. And when he came, I was frightened and fell on my face; but he said to me, "Understand, O son of man, that **the vision is for the time of the end.**" 19 And he said, "Look, I am making known to you what will happen in **the period of the wrath**, for it refers to **the appointed time of the end.** 26 The vision of the evenings and the mornings that has been told is true,[47] but **seal up the vision**,[48] for it refers to **many days from now.**"[49]

"The period of the wrath," has "the basic idea [of] experiencing or expressing intense anger. The word is parallel to *qāṣap*, except that its expression takes a more specific form, especially of denunciation."[50]

Daniel 12:4, 9, 13 Updated American standard Version (UASV)

4 But as for you, O Daniel, **conceal these words** and **seal up the book** <u>until</u> **the time of the end;** many shall run to and fro,[51] and **knowledge will increase.**" 9 He said, "Go

---

[47] Lit *truth*; Heb., *'emet*

[48] I.e., keep the vision secret; Heb., *satar*

[49] Lit *for to days many*; I.e., to the distant future

[50] Leon J. Wood, "568 זעם," ed. R. Laird Harris, Gleason L. Archer Jr., and Bruce K. Waltke, *Theological Wordbook of the Old Testament* (Chicago: Moody Press, 1999), 247.

[51] I.e. examine the book thoroughly

your way, Daniel, for the words are **shut up** and **sealed until the time of the end.** ¹³ But go your way till the end; and you shall rest and shall stand in your allotted place at **the end of the days.**"

The "time of wrath," connects it to "time of the end," and says: "It refers certainly to God's time of judgment on Israel at the time of Antiochus Epiphanes; but it refers also to God's future time of judgment during the great tribulation, in the last half of which the little horn of Daniel's first vision will bring even worse affliction" (Wood, Daniel, p. 106).

Campbell adds:

> It should also be noted that the expression "time of the end" occurs in Daniel 12:4 where it clearly means the time approaching Christ's Second Coming. The conclusion, then, is that we are to see an Antiochus Epiphanes a dread picture and symbol of Antichrist to come in the end time, or Tribulation" (Campbell, 126).

Kelly, West, Seiss, Pentecost, and Walvoord all support this dual reference approach to our passage. Walvoord says, "The entire chapter is historically filled in Antiochus, but to varying degrees foreshadowing typically the future world ruler who would dominate the situation at the end of the times of the Gentiles (Walvoord, Daniel, p. 196).

Archer, though hesitant, throws his considerable weight with this position as well:

> This interpretation has much to commend it, for Daniel makes clear through the assignment of the symbol of the "little horn" both to Antiochus of Kingdom III and to Antichrist of the latter-day phase of Kingdom IV that they bear to each other the relationship of type-antitype. Insofar as Epiphanes prefigured the determined

effort to be made by the Beast to destroy the biblical faith, that prophecy that described the career of Antiochus also pertained to "the time of the end." Every type has great relevance for its antitype. But the future dealings of Antichrist can only be conjectured or surmised. Therefore, our discussion will be confined to the established deeds of Antiochus Epiphanes (Archer, p. 106).[52]

Some Bible scholars rightly understand these references to end times, as an increased understanding of the prophecies in the book of Daniel at that times. "Understandably **Daniel** and his immediate readers could not have comprehended all the details of the prophecies given in this book (cf. v. 8). Not until history continued to unfold would many be able to understand these prophetic revelations. But God indicated that an increased understanding of what Daniel had written would come. People today, looking back over history, can see the significance of much of what Daniel predicted. And in **the time of the end** (cf. v. 9, and note "the end" and "the end of the days" in v. 13) the words of this book that have been sealed (kept intact) will be understood by **many** who will seek to gain **knowledge** from it. This will be in the Tribulation (cf. 11:40, "the time of the end"). Even though Daniel's people may not have fully understood this book's prophecies, the predictions did comfort them. They were assured that God will ultimately deliver Israel from the Gentiles and bring her into His covenanted promises."[53]

---

[52] Anders, Max. *Holman Old Testament Commentary - Daniel* (p. 232). B&H Publishing.

[53] J. Dwight Pentecost, "Daniel," in *The Bible Knowledge Commentary: An Exposition of the Scriptures*, ed. J. F. Walvoord and R. B. Zuck, vol. 1 (Wheaton, IL: Victor Books, 1985), 1373.

As to whether the Jews remained God's chosen people after the rejection of Jesus Christ, the Son of God, see this author's CPH Blog

It is "the third year of Cyrus king of Persia," and hence about 536 B.C.E., shortly after the Jews' return to Jerusalem. After a three-week fast, Daniel is by the bank of the Hiddekel (the Tigris) river. (Dan. 10:1, 4; Gen. 2:14) An angel appears to him and explains

Daniel 10:13-14 Updated American Standard Version (UASV)

¹³ The prince of the kingdom of Persia withstood me twenty-one days, but Michael, one of the chief princes, came to help me, for I was left there with the kings of Persia, ¹⁴ Now I have come to give you an understanding of what will happen to your people in the end of the days, for it is a vision yet for the days to come."

Chapter 10 of the book of Daniel precedes the final vision that was given to Daniel, the battles between The Kings of the South and the North.

Daniel 11:1 Updated American Standard Version (UASV)

11 "And as for me, in the first year of Darius the Mede [539/538 B.C.E.], I stood up to confirm and strengthen him.

This opening verse of chapter 11 could just as easily be seen as the closing verse of chapter 10. This is the angel still speaking here, not Daniel, and he is referring to his reign as the starting point of the prophetic message, as Darius was no longer living. God's angel continued,

Daniel 11:2 Updated American Standard Version (UASV)

---

article, MODERN ISRAEL IN BIBLE PROPHECY: Are the Natural Jews Today Still God's Chosen People?

https://christianpublishinghouse.co/2017/03/27/modern-israel-in-bible-prophecy-are-the-natural-jews-today-still-gods-chosen-people/

or http://tiny.cc/mdippy

² And now I will show you the truth. Behold, three more kings shall arise in Persia, and a fourth shall be far richer than all of them. And when he has become strong through his riches, he shall stir up all against the kingdom of Greece.

Just who were these Persian rulers?

The **three more kings shall arise in Persia** refer to Cyrus (539–529 B.C.E.), Cambyses (529–522 B.C.E.), and Darius I (Hystaspes) (521–486 B.C.), with Bardiya not being considered because he ruled for only seven months. The fourth was the son and successor of Darius, Xerxes I (485–465 B.C.). He was the King Ahasuerus who married Esther, who was richer than all who preceded him. With his wealth and power, he embarked on a campaign against Greece.

Daniel 11:3-4 Updated American Standard Version (UASV)

³ And a mighty king will arise, and he will rule with great dominion and do as he wills. ⁴ And as soon as he has **stood up**,[54] his kingdom shall be broken and divided toward the four winds of heaven, but not to **his posterity, nor according to the authority** with which he ruled, for his kingdom shall be plucked up and go to others besides these.

Twenty-year-old Alexander "**stood up**" as king of Macedonia in 336 B.C.E. He did become "a mighty king," known the world over today as Alexander the Great. "Between 334 and 330 B. Alexander conquered Asia Minor, Syria, Egypt, and the land of the Medo-Persian Empire. His conquests extended as far as India."[55] Alexander was not quite 33 years old when malaria

---

[54] Or *risen*

[55] J. Dwight Pentecost, "Daniel," in *The Bible Knowledge Commentary: An Exposition of the Scriptures*, ed. J. F. Walvoord and R. B. Zuck, vol. 1 (Wheaton, IL: Victor Books, 1985), 1367–1368.

coupled with alcoholism took his life in Babylon in 323 B.C.E.

The great empire of Alexander the Great was not passed onto "**his posterity**." Alexander's brother Philip III Arrhidaeus reign lasted less than seven years, as he and his wife Eurydice were murdered at the order of Olympias, Alexander's mother, in 317 B.C.E. Alexander's son Alexander IV ruled until 311 B.C.E., wherein he was killed at the hands of Cassander, one of his father's generals. Alexander has an illegitimate son Heracles, who then sought to rule in his father's name but was murdered in 309 B.C.E. Thus, we see that Alexander the Great rose up as a mighty king and ruled with great dominion, yet his kingdom was short lived but was not to go to his posterity because they could not rule with his authority.

Rather Alexander's kingdom was literally "broken and divided toward the four winds of heaven," that is, "his kingdom was divided among his four generals (cf. 8:22): Seleucus (over Syria and Mesopotamia), Ptolemy (over Egypt), Lysimacus (over Thrace and portions of Asia Minor), and Cassander (over Macedonia and Greece). This division was anticipated through the four heads of the leopard (7:6) and the four prominent horns on the goat (8:8)."[56]

Daniel 11:5-6 Updated American Standard Version (UASV)

[5] "Then the king of the south will be strong, but one of his princes will be stronger than he and will rule, and his authority will be a greater dominion. [6] After some years they will make an alliance, and the daughter of the king of the south will come to the king of the north to make an agreement. But she will not retain the strength of her arm, and he and his arm will not endure, but she will be given

---

[56] J. Dwight Pentecost, "Daniel," in *The Bible Knowledge Commentary: An Exposition of the Scriptures*, ed. J. F. Walvoord and R. B. Zuck, vol. 1 (Wheaton, IL: Victor Books, 1985), 1368.

up, along with those who brought her in, he who fathered her, and he who supported her in those times.

The titles "the king of the south" and "the king of the north" refer to kings south and north of Daniel's people, who had been freed from Babylonian captivity and was now restored to the land of Judah. The first "king of the south" was a general who had served under Alexander, Ptolemy I Soter of Egypt (304-283 B.C.E.). Another general of Alexander was Syrian King Seleucus I Nicator (304-281 B.C.E) "and his authority will be a greater dominion," who assumed the role of "the king of the north."

From the initial "king of the south" and the "king of the north" "conflicts arose between the kingdoms of the Ptolemies (Egypt) and the Seleucids (Syria)."[57] Because Antiochus I, the son and successor of his father Seleucus I Nicator did not wage a significant war against the king of the south, the prophecy did not mention him. However, his successor, Antiochus II, fought a very long war against Ptolemy II, the son of Ptolemy I. Therefore, Ptolemy II and Antiochus II constituted the king of the south and the king of the north respectively. Antiochus II married Laodice, and they had a son named Seleucus II, while Ptolemy II had a daughter named Berenice. In about 250 B.C.E., "the daughter of the king of the south will come to the king of the north to make an agreement." In order to make this alliance, Antiochus II divorced his wife Laodice and married Berenice, "the daughter of the king of the south."

We are told (11:6) she will not retain the strength of her arm, that is the supporting power of her father, Ptolemy II. When he died in 246 B.C.E., she did no longer had the support and power of her father, as his "arm will not endure" with her husband. Bernice "will be given up,

---

[57] Stephen R. Miller, *Daniel*, vol. 18, The New American Commentary (Nashville: Broadman & Holman Publishers, 1994), 293.

along with those who brought her in, he who fathered her, and he who supported her in those times.

But, and he and his arm will not endure, but she shall be given up, along with those who brought her in, he who fathered her, and he who supported her in those times. Antiochus II rejected Bernice; after that, he remarried Laodice and named their son as his successor. As Laodice had planned, she succeeded "in murdering Antiochus, Berenice, and their child. Thus their 'power' did 'not last.' Laodice then ruled as queen regent during the minority of her son, Seleucus II Callinicus (246–226 B.C.)."[58] J. Dwight Pentecost tells us, "Laodice, whom Antiochus had divorced in order to marry Berenice, had Berenice killed (she was **handed over**). Laodice then poisoned Antiochus II and made her son, Seleucus II Callinicus, king (246–227)."[59] How would the next Ptolemaic king respond to all of this?

Daniel 11:7-9 Updated American Standard Version (UASV)

7 "And **one from the sprout of her roots** will stand up in his position, and he will come to the army and come against **the fortress of the king of the north**, and he will deal with them and will prevail. 8 Also their gods, with their **metal images**,[60] with their precious vessels of silver and of gold, he will take captive to Egypt; and for some years he will stand off from the king of the north, 9 Then the latter will come into the realm of the king of the south but will return to his own land.

"One from the sprout" of Berenice's parents, or "roots," was her brother. At his father's death, he 'stood

---

[58] IBID, 293–294.

[59] J. Dwight Pentecost, "Daniel," in *The Bible Knowledge Commentary: An Exposition of the Scriptures*, ed. J. F. Walvoord and R. B. Zuck, vol. 1 (Wheaton, IL: Victor Books, 1985), 1368.

[60] Or *molten statues*

up' as the king of the south, the Egyptian Pharaoh Ptolemy III Euergetes (246–221 B.C.E.). He wasted no time in the vengeance of his sister's murder. He attacked Syrian King Seleucus II, who Laodice had used to murder Berenice and her son, he came against "the fortress of the king of the north." Ptolemy III took the fortified part of Antioch, capturing the major cities of Antioch and Seleucia and dealt a deathblow to Laodice.

Some 200 years earlier, Persian King Cambyses II had conquered Egypt and carried home Egyptian gods, "their metal images" or "their molten statues." Here we have Ptolemy III plundering the former royal capital Susa, where he recovered these "gods," taking them captive, carrying home the spoils of war. He also brought back as spoils of war a great many "precious vessels of silver and of gold." And Ptolemy III "for some years he will stand off from the king of the north," to quell revolt at home.

However, the king of the north, Syrian King Seleucus II, attempted to strike back. "In 242 Seleucus II attempted to invade Egypt but was forced to withdraw. For the rest of his reign, he was too busy with other problems to engage in further conflict with Egypt."[61] Seleucus II with only a small remnant of his army was forced to "return to his own land." At his death, his son Seleucus III succeeded him. "This was the beginning of the seesaw battle between the two nations."[62]

---

[61] John H Walton, *Zondervan Illustrated Bible Backgrounds Commentary (Old Testament): Isaiah, Jeremiah, Lamentations, Ezekiel, Daniel*, vol. 4 (Grand Rapids, MI: Zondervan, 2009), 562.

[62] Walvoord, John. Daniel (The John Walvoord Prophecy Commentaries) (Kindle Location 6113). Moody Publishers.

CHAPTER 4 The Kings of the South and the North

Daniel 11:10-20 (226 – 175 B.C.E.)

Daniel 11:10-13 Updated American Standard Version (UASV)

¹⁰ "His sons will wage war and assemble a multitude of great forces, which will keep coming and overflow and pass through, and again will wage war up to his fortress. ¹¹ Then the king of the south, moved with rage, will come out and fight against the king of the north. And he will raise a great multitude, but it will be given into his hand. ¹² And when the multitude is **taken away**, his heart will be lifted up, and he will cast down tens of thousands, but he will not prevail. ¹³ For the king of the north will again raise a multitude, greater than the former, and after some years[63] he will come on with a great army and many supplies.

Seleucus III reign was short-lived, for in less than three years he was assassinated. His brother, Antiochus III, came to the Syrian throne. After he had dealt with the rebellions in Media and Asia Minor, Antiochus III gathered a great military force for an attack on the king of the south, who was by then Ptolemy IV. "Antiochus III … was called the "Great" because of his military successes, and in 219–218 B.C. he campaigned in Phoenicia and Palestine, part of the Ptolemaic Empire ("as far as his [the king of the South's] fortress")."[64]

---

[63] Lit *at the end of the times, years*

[64] Stephen R. Miller, *Daniel*, vol. 18, The New American Commentary (Nashville: Broadman & Holman Publishers, 1994), 294.

Massing a military force of 75,000, the king of the south, Ptolemy IV, moved northward against the enemy, the king of the north. We are told that the Syrian king of the north, Antiochus III raised "a great multitude [68,000], but it will be given into his hand." Antiochus III suffered defeat at the coastal city of Raphia, not far from Egypt's border.[65] A "multitude is taken away" by Ptolemy IV, the king of the south, 10,000 Syrian infantrymen and 300 cavalrymen into death and he took 4,000 as prisoners. The kings then made a truce agreement whereby Antiochus III kept his Syrian seaport of Seleucia but lost Phoenicia and Coele-Syria. Because of this victory, the 'heart of the Egyptian king of the south was lifted up,' especially toward the one true God of the Jews. Judah remained under the control of Ptolemy IV. Nevertheless, he did not take advantage of the strong position that he held, trying to stay on top of this victory against the Syrian king of the north, so in the end 'he did not prevail.

But rather, Ptolemy IV turned to a life of depravity and corruption, and his five-year-old son, Ptolemy V, became the next king of the south some years before the death of Antiochus III. "fifteen years later (202 b.c.) Antiochus III again invaded Ptolemaic territories with a huge army. The occasion for this invasion was the death of Ptolemy IV in 203 B.C. and the crowning of his young son (between four and six years of age), Ptolemy V Epiphanes (203–181 B.C.), as the new king. Antiochus III took full advantage of the opportunity and attacked

---

[65] "According to Polybius, Ptolemy's forces consisted of 70,000 infantry, 5,000 cavalry, and 73 elephants; whereas Antiochus's army had 62,000 infantry, 6,000 cavalry, and 102 elephants. When the battle ended [in 217 B.C.], Ptolemy had won a great victory over the Syrians at Raphia (located in Palestine)." – Stephen R. Miller, Daniel, vol. 18, The New American Commentary (Nashville: Broadman & Holman Publishers, 1994), 295.

Phoenicia and Palestine; by 201 B.C. the fortress in Gaza had fallen to the Syrians."[66]

Daniel 11:14 Updated American Standard Version (UASV)

[14] "In those times many will rise against the king of the south, and the **violent among your own people** will lift themselves up in order to fulfill the vision, but they will stumble.[67]

"In those times many [did] rise against the king of the south." Not only did the king of the south have to face the forces of Antiochus III, as well as his Macedonian ally, but the young king also had many problems at home in Egypt. The young king of the south was facing a revolt because his guardian Agathocles, who ruled in his name, dealt haughtily with the Egyptians. Daniel 11:14b tells us "the violent among your own people will lift themselves up in order to fulfill the vision." However, this "vision" of ending the Gentile dominion of their homeland was false and they 'were going to stumble.'

Daniel 11:15-16 Updated American Standard Version (UASV)

[15] And the king of the north will come and throw up a siege rampart and capture a **fortified city**. And the arms of the south will not stand, nor will his select men; and they will have no power to stand. [16] The one coming against him will do as he pleases, and no one will stand before him; he will **stand in the land of the beauty**,[68] with destruction in his hand.

---

[66] Stephen R. Miller, *Daniel*, vol. 18, The New American Commentary (Nashville: Broadman & Holman Publishers, 1994), 295.

[67] Or *will fail*

[68] I.e. Palestine

Military forces under Ptolemy V, or "arms of the south," surrendered to assault from the north. At Paneas (Caesarea Philippi), Antiochus III drove Egypt's General Scopas and 10,000 "select men," into Sidon, "a fortified city." There Antiochus III would "throw up a siege rampart," taking that Phoenician seaport in 199 B.C.E. "He then retreated to Sidon on the Phoenician coast. Antiochus's forces pursued the Egyptians and besieged Sidon. General Scopas finally surrendered in 198 B.C.E."[69] Antiochus would "do as he pleases" because "no one [the Egyptian king of the south] will stand before him." Antiochus III then marched against Jerusalem, the capital of "the land of the beauty," namely, Judah, "with destruction in his hand."

Daniel 11:17 Updated American Standard Version (UASV)

[17] He will **set his face** to come **with the full force of his kingdom**, and there will be **equitable terms**; and he will perform them; he will give him the daughter of women to destroy her. But she will not stand for him, or be for him.

The king of the north, Antiochus III, "set his face" to completely control Egypt "with the full force of his kingdom." But rather he chose in the end to make "equitable terms" of peace with the king of the south, Ptolemy V. When Antiochus III and King Philip V of Macedonia join in a league or alliance against the young Egyptian king, attempting to take over his territories, the guardians of Ptolemy V went to Rome for protection, causing Antiochus III to change his plan. In this alliance of peace Antiochus III gave his daughter, Cleopatra I "the daughter of women," in marriage to Ptolemy V, hoping his daughter would be an inside spy so as to make Egypt subject to Syria. However, the scheme failed because

---

[69] Stephen R. Miller, *Daniel*, vol. 18, The New American Commentary (Nashville: Broadman & Holman Publishers, 1994), 296.

Cleopatra I "[would] not stand for him, or be for him," but rather she sided with her husband. She "became staunchly loyal to her husband, even encouraging him to make an alliance with Rome against her father."[70]

Gleason L. Archer offers insight into this masterful scheme gone bad, "As it turned out, however, after the marriage finally took place in 195 [B.C.E.], Cleopatra became completely sympathetic to her husband, Ptolemy V, and the Ptolemaic cause, much to the disappointment of her father, Antiochus. Therefore, when she gave birth to a royal heir, who became Ptolemy VI, this gave no particular advantage or political leverage to her father. When Ptolemy V died in 181, Cleopatra was appointed queen regent by the Egyptian government, because they all loved and appreciated her loyalty to their cause. But she herself died not long after, and this meant the end of all possible Seleucid influence on Egyptian affairs. Yet by that time Antiochus himself, who died in 187 B.C., was gone." (Archer, The Expositor's Bible Commentary, Vol. 7: Daniel and the Minor Prophets 1985, 132-33)

Daniel 11:18-19 Updated American Standard Version (UASV)

[18] Afterward he will **turn his face back to the coastlands** and will capture many. But a **commander** will put a stop to his reproach against him; he will turn his reproach upon him. [19] Then he will turn his face back toward the fortresses of his own land, but he will stumble and fall, and will not be found.

Antiochus would "turn his face back to the coastlands. The "coastlands" were those of Macedonia, Greece, and Asia Minor. Antiochus is an effort to repeat the accomplishments of Alexander the Great, sought to

---

[70] John H Walton, *Zondervan Illustrated Bible Backgrounds Commentary (Old Testament): Isaiah, Jeremiah, Lamentations, Ezekiel, Daniel*, vol. 4 (Grand Rapids, MI: Zondervan, 2009), 564.

conquer and control Greece. However, Greece had other plans, as they turned to Rome for help. Rome formally declared war on him. This put Antiochus in battle on several fronts: Macedonia, Rome, and Greece. "The Romans defeated [Antiochus] at Thermopylae in 191 [B.C.E.] and then crushed him at the Battle of Magnesia in 190 [B.C.E.]. This forced him back east across the Taurus Mountains. The commander who defeated him was Lucius Scipio. By the Treaty of Apmea in 189 [B.C.E.] Antiochus became a vassal of Rome, had to send twenty hostages to Rome, and paid a huge indemnity. This left him humiliated and short of funds."[71]

Daniel 11:20 Updated American Standard Version (UASV)

20 "Then there will stand up in his position one who causes an exactor to pass through the glory of his kingdom, but in a few days he will be broken, though not in anger nor in warfare.

God's angel foretold, "There will stand up in his position [*that of Antiochus III*] one who causes an exactor [the tax collector Heliodorus] to pass through the glory of his kingdom, but in a few days he will be broken, though not in anger nor in warfare." (Daniel 11:20) The one who was to "standing up" in this manner was Seleucus IV Philopator. (187–175 B.C.E.) "Seleucus IV reigned only 'a few years' and was not killed by an angry mob ("in anger") like his father or 'in battle.' Heliodorus, his tax collector and prime minister, evidently seeking to gain the throne for himself, poisoned the king (possibly abetted by Antiochus IV)."[72]

---

[71] John H Walton, *Zondervan Illustrated Bible Backgrounds Commentary (Old Testament): Isaiah, Jeremiah, Lamentations, Ezekiel, Daniel*, vol. 4 (Grand Rapids, MI: Zondervan, 2009), 564.

[72] Stephen R. Miller, *Daniel*, vol. 18, The New American Commentary (Nashville: Broadman & Holman Publishers, 1994), 297.

CHAPTER 5 The Kings of the South and the North

Daniel 11:21-35 (175 – 164 B.C.E.)

Daniel 11:21 Updated American Standard Version (UASV)

²¹ And there will stand up in his place **a despicable one**, and they have not conferred the majesty of the kingdom; and he will come in during a time of security and seize the kingdom by intrigue.

Antiochus IV Epiphanes (175–163 B.C.E.) had been a political hostage in Rome Since the defeat of Antiochus III at Magnesia. However, in 175 B.C.E. the oldest son of Seleucus IV, Demetrius I, was sent to Rome in replacement of Antiochus IV. Arriving home, Antiochus IV assumed power as a co-ruler with Antiochus III, the latter here dying in 170 C.E., leaving Antiochus IV to rule alone on the throne. Antiochus IV Epiphanes was certainly "a despicable one," for his severe persecution of the Jews, massacring thousands, and he became the greatest threat to the pure worship within Israel since Abraham left Haran for the Promise Land. Antiochus IV assumed the title Epiphanes, which means the "Manifest One," or "Illustrious One," clearly evidencing his haughty spirit.

Daniel 11:22-24 Updated American Standard Version (UASV)

²² Armies shall be **utterly swept away** before him and broken, even **the leader of the covenant**. ²³ And after an alliance is made with him, he will act deceitfully, and he will rise and he will become powerful by means of a little nation. ²⁴ **In a time of tranquility** he will enter the richest parts of the province, and he will accomplish what his

fathers and their fathers have not done; he will distribute plunder, booty and possessions among them, and he will **devise his schemes against strongholds**, but only for a time.

At the tender age of six Ptolemy VII (Philometor) took the throne at the age of six under control of his mother Cleopatra in 181 B.C.E., as it was she who controlled the kingdom. Shortly after that he moves on Palestine with a huge military force and was soundly defeated by Antiochus Epiphanes who destroyed, in the process, "the leader of the covenant." The Egyptian armies were utterly swept away by the invading forces of Antiochus as if it were by a flood. Antiochus gave the order to murder "the leader of the covenant, Onias III, which was carried out by his own defecting brother Menelaus about 171 B.C.E.

Walvoord tells us, "The reference to the "prince of the covenant" prophesied the deposing and eventual murder of the high priest Onias, which was ordered by Antiochus in 172 B.C. and indicates the troublesome times of his reign.39 The high priest bore the title "prince of the covenant" because he was de facto the head of the theocracy at that time. In 11:28 and 11:32 the term "covenant" is used for the Jewish state. Antiochus sold the office of high priest to Onias's brother, Jason, who sought to Hellenize the Jewish state."[73]

However, Stephen R. Miller sees the "prince of the covenant differently, saying, "Montgomery identifies the "prince [leader] of the covenant" as the high priest Onias III, who was assassinated in 170 B.C. (Daniel, 451; also, Lacocque, Daniel, 226; Hartman and Di Lella, Daniel, 295; Wood, Daniel, 295). In context with the defeat of the Egyptian army, it is best to see this "prince" as its leader. The entire phrase is indefinite and can be rendered 'a

---

[73] Walvoord, John. Daniel (The John Walvoord Prophecy Commentaries) (Kindle Locations 6232-6237). Moody Publishers.

prince of a covenant.' He goes on to say, "Ptolemy is called 'a prince [leader] of the covenant' because he agreed (made a covenant) to become an ally of Antiochus if the Syrians would help him regain his throne in Egypt, which had been taken by his younger brother, Ptolemy VII Euergetes II (Physcon). Antiochus was delighted to make such a pact, for he felt that it would give him a foothold in Egypt. So with Syrian help, Ptolemy regained his throne. Later Ptolemy broke this agreement and allied himself with his brother Ptolemy VII to dislodge Antiochus's troops from Pelusium, a fortress on the border of Egypt."[74]

In verse 24 we find Antiochus Epiphanes taking from the rich Egyptian places he could strike and giving to the poor and his own forces, to gain support and strengthen his control over the empire, as well as build up to take over Egypt.

Daniel 11:25-28 Updated American Standard Version (UASV)

[25] And he will **stir up his power and his heart against the king of the south** with a great army; and the king of the south shall wage war with an exceedingly great and mighty army, but he will not stand, for plots will be devised against him. [26] Even **those who eat** his food will break him; and his army will be swept away, and many will fall down slain. [27] As for both kings, their heart will be inclined to do what is evil, and **they will speak lies** to each other at the same table; but it will not succeed, for the end is still to come at the appointed time. [28] Then he will return to his land with many possessions, but his heart will be set **against the holy covenant**, and he will take action and he will return to his own land.

Antiochus set out to attacked Ptolemy VI Philometer in 170 B.C.E., the king of Egypt (c. 186 – 145 B.C.E.), who

---

[74] Stephen R. Miller, *Daniel*, vol. 18, The New American Commentary (Nashville: Broadman & Holman Publishers, 1994), 299.

had become his enemy. Antiochus was able to defeat an Egyptian army near Pelusium, and then he captured Memphis but was not in a position to take Alexandria. Miller tells us that "Cumulatively these things prevented Ptolemy from successfully 'standing' against the Syrians. 'Those who eat from the king's provisions' (v. 26) were Ptolemy's trusted counselors, who unwisely urged the young king to recapture Syria and Palestine, thus incurring the wrath of Antiochus."[75]

Antiochus Epiphanes 'spoke lies,' as he pretended to help Ptolemy Philometer regain the throne in Egypt, which was then by Ptolemy Euergetes. Both kings "they will speak lies to each other at the same table." Antiochus had Philometer as king at Memphis, while he had Euergetes reigned at Alexandria. However, things did not go as planned because the two Egyptian kings decided up a joint rule, which greatly angered the Syrian. "Antiochus's successful first campaign against Egypt in 169 B.C. is the background for v. 28. After plundering Egypt, the king returned home by way of Palestine and found an insurrection in progress (cf. 1 Macc. 1:16–28; 2 Macc. 5:1–11). He put down the rebellion, massacring eighty thousand men, women, and children (2 Macc. 5:12–14) and then looted the temple with the help of the evil high priest, Menelaus (cf. 2 Macc. 5:15–21). The persecution of the Jews by this evil tyrant had now escalated to calamitous proportions."[76] These sources outside of the Scriptures are not inspired books of the Bible. However, First and Second Maccabees are historical accounts of the Jewish struggle for independence during the second-century B.C.E. These are the most valuable of the Old

---

[75] Stephen R. Miller, *Daniel*, vol. 18, The New American Commentary (Nashville: Broadman & Holman Publishers, 1994), 300.

[76] Stephen R. Miller, *Daniel*, vol. 18, The New American Commentary (Nashville: Broadman & Holman Publishers, 1994), 300.

Testament Apocryphal works because of the historical information they supply for this period.

Daniel 11:29-30 Updated American Standard Version (UASV)

[29] "At the appointed time he will return and he will **come into the south**, but it will not be as it was before. [30] For **ships** of Kittim[77] will **come against him**; therefore he will be disheartened and will return and become enraged at the holy covenant and take action; so he will come back and show regard for those who forsake the holy covenant.

Here again, for the third time, we find Antiochus invading Egypt against the co-rulers about 168 B.C.E., "but it will not be as it was before, for a Roman fleet of ships from Cyprus sided with Egypt this time, frustrating the attack by Antiochus. "When he tried to play for time, the Roman envoy drew a circle around him in the sand and insisted on an answer before he stepped out of it. Humiliated, he withdrew from Egypt."[78] Antiochus left Egypt in a fit of rage, taking his anger out on the Israelites as he headed back home. He despised the Jews God and their Mosaic Law, so he showed favor to the apostate Jews, yes Antiochus showed "regard for those who forsake the holy covenant."

Miller tells us that "In 167 B.C., Antiochus turned his humiliation into anger against the Jewish people ("the holy covenant") once more (cf. 1 Macc 1:29–40; 2 Macc 6:1–6). He sent Apollonius (2 Macc 5:23–26), the head of his mercenaries and the "chief collector of tribute" (1 Macc 1:29), to Jerusalem. Apollonius pretended to come in

---

[77] I.e. Cyprus

[78] John H Walton, *Zondervan Illustrated Bible Backgrounds Commentary (Old Testament): Isaiah, Jeremiah, Lamentations, Ezekiel, Daniel*, vol. 4 (Grand Rapids, MI: Zondervan, 2009), 565.

peace, but on the Sabbath Day, he suddenly attacked, massacring many people and plundering the city (cf. 1 Macc. 1:30–32; cf. 2 Macc. 5:25–26). But he rewarded those apostate Jews like the high priest Menelaus, who supported his Hellenistic policies (cf. 1 Macc. 1:1, 43; 2 Macc. 4:7–17)."[79]

Daniel 11:31-32 Updated American Standard Version (UASV)

[31] Forces from him will stand up, **desecrate the sanctuary** fortress, and do away with the continual sacrifice. And they will set up the **abomination**[80] **that causes desolation.** [32] And those who act wickedly against the covenant, he will pollute by means of smooth words; but **the people who know their God** will prevail and act effectively.

The soldier of Antiochus worked in conjunction with the apostate Jews, guarding the temple, halting pure worship of the one true God. In addition, other Antiochus troops were sent out on the Sabbath to slaughter Jewish men, women, and children. The soldiers "desecrate the sanctuary," banned circumcision, and done away with away with "the continual sacrifice" (i.e., daily sacrifices), as well as offering up in sacrifice a big on God's altar. (1 Macc. 1:44–54) Moreover, on Chislev (Dec. 15, 167 B.C.E.) the Syrians even made compulsory worship of an idol statue in honor of the Olympian god Zeus in the temple. The Jews called it "the abomination that causes desolation." **Abomination:** (Heb. *shiqquts*) It means abhorrence, an object to abhor, horror, monster, filth. The sense of *shiqquts* is a detestable thing, also implying that it can

---

[79] Stephen R. Miller, *Daniel*, vol. 18, The New American Commentary (Nashville: Broadman & Holman Publishers, 1994), 301.

[80] **Abomination:** (Heb. *shiqquts*) It means abhorrence, an object to abhor, horror, monster, filth. The sense of *shiqquts* is a detestable thing, also implying that it can make a person unclean. – 2 Ki 23:13; Ez. 5:11; 11:21; Dan. 9:27; 11:31; Hos. 9:10.

make a person unclean. In other words, the Syrians ruined pure worship of the one true God in the temple by introducing an abhorrent, detestable, filthy object (the Olympian god Zeus) in the temple. The soldiers of Antiochus further profaned the temple by spreading sow's broth on the altar. (1 Macc. 1:44-54) Both Daniel and Jesus said this barbarism was only a preview of the abomination that was to come – Daniel 9:27; Matthew 24:15.

The Abomination of Desolation

Matthew 24:15 Update American Standard Version (UASV)

15 "Therefore when you see the abomination of desolation, which was spoken of through Daniel the prophet, standing in the holy place (let the reader understand),

Matthew 24:13 reads, "But **the one who endures to the end** will be saved." Matthew 24:14 said, "this gospel of the kingdom will be proclaimed throughout the whole world as a testimony to all nations, **and then the end will come**." Matthew 24:15 begins with the Greek word *hotan* "whenever" followed by *oun* "therefore, which reads in English, "Therefore when," which connects what preceded, **"the end,"** and leads into what follows. Let us take a moment to investigate verse 15.

In verse 3-14, Jesus outlined the signs of "the end of the age." Here in Mathew 24:15, Jesus begins with **"Therefore when** you see the abomination of desolation, which was spoken of through Daniel the prophet, standing in the holy place (let the reader understand)." If we look at the corresponding accounts in Mark and Luke, they offer us additional insights. Mark 13:14 says, "standing where it ought not to be." Luke 21:20 adds Jesus' words, "But when you see Jerusalem surrounded by armies, then know[81] that

---

[81] Or *then recognize*

its desolation has come near." The complete picture is an "abomination" "standing in the holy place," i.e., "where it ought not be," namely, "Jerusalem surrounded by armies,"

This is a reference to the Roman army, which assaulted Jerusalem and its temple starting in 66 C.E., under General Cestus Gallus. The temple was the "holy place," and the abomination was the Roman army "standing where it ought not to be." As for the "desolation," this came in 70 C.E. when General Titus of the Roman army completely desolated Jerusalem and its temple. Specifically, what was this "abomination"? Moreover, in what sense was it "standing in the holy place"?

Jesus had urged the readers to *understand*. What was it that they were to *understand*? They were to *understand* that "which was spoken of through Daniel the prophet," i.e., Daniel 9:27. Part "b" of verse 27 reads "And upon the wing of abominations shall come the one causing desolation, even until a complete destruction, one that is decreed, is poured out on the one causing desolation." – Daniel 9:26-27; see also Daniel 11:31; 12:11.

> The *abomination of desolation* is an expression that recurs in Daniel with some variation in wording (Daniel 8:13; 9:27; 11:31; 12:11), where most scholars agree that there is a reference to the desecration perpetrated by Antiochus Epiphanes when he built an altar to Zeus in the temple and offered swine and other unclean animals on it as sacrifices (cf. 1 Macc. 1:41–61).[82]

We can have it but one of two ways, as Jesus' words were a clear reference to the Roman armies of 66–70 C.E.

---

[82] Leon Morris, *The Gospel According to Matthew*, The Pillar New Testament Commentary (Grand Rapids, MI; Leicester, England: W.B. Eerdmans; Inter-Varsity Press, 1992), 603.

STANDARD OF THE 10TH ROMAN LEGION This Legion attacked and destroyed Jerusalem in the Jewish War (A.D. 70).

It may very well be that Daniel's prophecy points to Antiochus Epiphanes "who in 167 [B.C.E., 200-years before Jesus uttered his prophecy] plundered the temple, ordered the sacrificial system to cease, and polluted the altar of the Lord by turning it into a pagan altar, where unclean sacrifices were offered to pagan deities."[83] This would be no different from Matthew referring to Hosea 11:1 (When Israel was a child ... and out of Egypt I called my son). In that case, Matthew did not use Hosea's intended meaning, but carried out an *Inspired Sensus Plenior Application*, by having a whole other meaning, an entirely different meaning for those words, making them applicable to Jesus being called back out of Egypt. It could be that Jesus used Daniel's prophecy about Antiochus Epiphanes, and gave is an *Inspired Sensus Plenior Application*, by having a whole other meaning, a completely different meaning for those words, making them applicable to the Roman armies desolating Jerusalem between 66 and 70 C.E. Then, again, it could be that was what Daniel was pointing to all along, and Jesus used Daniel's words in a grammatical-historical application. Either way, it still comes out the same.

> During the days of the Maccabees this expression was used to describe the sacrilege of Antiochus IV Epiphanes, the Seleucid king who decreed that an altar to Olympian Zeus and

---

[83] Larry Chouinard, *Matthew*, The College Press NIV Commentary (Joplin, MO: College Press, 1997), Mt 24:15.

perhaps a statue of himself were to be erected in the temple on 15 Chislev, 167 b.c.: "They erected a desolating sacrilege on the altar of burnt offering. They also built altars in the surrounding towns of Judah." Antiochus further decreed that the Sabbath and other festal observances were to be profaned, that circumcision was to be abolished, and that swine and other unclean animals were to be sacrificed in the temple (cf. 1 Macc. 1:41–50). This was one of the lowest points of Jewish history and was considered by many the primary focus of Daniel's prophecy. Jesus now quotes Daniel directly to clarify that the fulfillment of the "abomination that causes desolation" is yet future.[84]

When Jesus uttered those words of verse 15, the abomination of desolation was yet to appear. Jesus was clearly pointing to the Roman army of 66 C.E., with its distinctive standards, which were idols to the Romans and the empire, but an abomination to the Jews.

Judæa was under the charge of a Roman official, a subordinate of the governor of the Roman province of Syria, who held a relation to that functionary similar to that which the Governor of Bombay holds to the Governor-General at Calcutta. Roman soldiers paraded the streets of Jerusalem; **Roman standards** waved over the fastnesses of the country; Roman tax-gatherers sat at the gate of every town. To the Sanhedrin, the supreme Jewish organ of government, only a shadow of power was still conceded, its presidents, the high priests, being mere puppets of Rome, set up and put down with the utmost caprice. So low had the proud nation fallen whose ideal it had ever been to rule the world, and whose patriotism

---

[84] Clinton E. Arnold, *Zondervan Illustrated Bible Backgrounds Commentary: Matthew, Mark, Luke*, vol. 1 (Grand Rapids, MI: Zondervan, 2002), 148.

was a religious and national passion as intense and unquenchable as ever burned in any country.[85]

In verse 32 we are told "but the people who know their God will prevail and act effectively," which referred to the Hasmonaeans. A dynamic Jewish leader, Judah Maccabee, of a family known as the Hasmonaeans, led a rebel army that freed the temple from Greek hands. Possibly because of Judah's military ability, he was called Maccabee, meaning "hammer." Maccabee was a "name given to the family of Mattathias, a faithful priest, who led in a revolt (Maccabean War) against the Hellenizing influences of the Seleucid King Antiochus Epiphanes in about 168 B.C.E."[86]

The Hasmonaean Dynasty

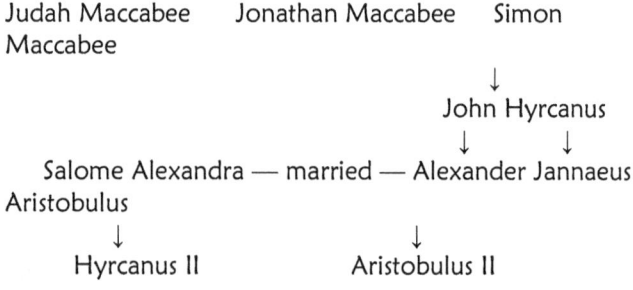

II. Maccabean Revolt

A. Antiochus's Revenge (168–166 B.C.) In the winter of 169/168, the rival brothers Ptolemy VI and Ptolemy VIII agreed to end their dispute and united against their uncle Antiochus IV. Thus, in the spring of

---

[85] James Stalker, *The Life of Jesus Christ* (Chicago: Henry A. Sumner and Company, 1882), 30–31.

[86] Chad Brand et al., eds., "Maccabees," *Holman Illustrated Bible Dictionary* (Nashville, TN: Holman Bible Publishers, 2003), 1063.

168 Antiochus IV invaded Egypt a second time. He captured Memphis, but when he attempted to subdue Eleusis, a suburb of Alexandria, the Roman general Popillius Laenas gave him an ultimatum from the senate to withdraw immediately from Egypt (cf. Polybius xxix.2.1–4; 27.1–8; Livy xlv.12.1–6; Diodorus xxxi.2; Velleius Paterculus i.10.1f; Appian Syr 66; Justinus xxxiv.3; Dnl. 11:28–30). Antiochus immediately retreated, having learned of Rome's power as its hostage for fourteen years.

Embittered, Antiochus decided to establish Palestine as a buffer state between him and the Roman encroachment (Polybius xxix.27.9; Dnl. 11:30). He destroyed the walls of Jerusalem and refortified the old Davidic city making it the pagan stronghold (Acra). Considering himself Zeus Epiphanes, he ordered a vigorous hellenization program that would exterminate the Jewish religion. He forbade the Jews to celebrate the sabbath and feasts, to offer the traditional sacrifices, and to perform circumcision, and he ordered the destruction of the copies of the Torah.

The Jews were ordered to offer up unclean sacrifices on idolatrous altars and to eat swine's flesh (2 Macc. 6:18). The climactic act was on 25 Chislev (Dec. 16) 167, when the temple of Jerusalem became the place of worship of the Olympian Zeus. The altar of Zeus was erected on the altar of burnt offering, and swine's flesh was offered on it (Dnl. 11:31f.; 1 Macc. 1:41–64; 2 Macc. 6:1–11).

B. Mattathias (166 B.C.) In every village of Palestine sacrifice was to be offered to the heathen gods under the supervision of imperial representatives. In the village of Modein (27 km, 17 mi, NW of Jerusalem) an aged priest named Mattathias defied the command of Antiochus IV's legate to offer the sacrifice on the heathen altar. When another Jew was about to comply,

Mattathias killed him and the legate and destroyed the altar, saying, "Let everyone who is zealous for the law and supports the covenant come out with me" (1 Macc. 2:15–27; Josephus Ant. xii.6.1f [265–272]; cf. Dnl. 11:32–35). Mattathias, his five sons (John, Simon, Judas, Eleazar, and Jonathan) and many other Jews fled to the mountains; this marked the beginning of the Maccabean revolt.

Mattathias and his followers exhorted Jews everywhere to join their struggle against hellenization. They gained the support of the Hasidim, those who were faithful to the Torah. They tore down heathen altars and circumcised children who had been left uncircumcised. After a long life, Mattathias died in 166. He exhorted his sons to continue the struggle and appointed his third son Judas as the commander of the war (1 Macc. 2:42–70; Josephus Ant. xii.6.2–4 [273–286]).

C. Judas Maccabeus (166–160 B.C.)

1. Rededication of the Temple (166–164 B.C.) The selection of Judas to carry on the struggle was the right one, for he proved to be a very capable leader in defeating the Seleucids. In his first year he defeated the Syrian governors Apollonius and Seron (1 Macc. 3:10–26; Josephus Ant. xii.7.1 [287–292]).

Part of Antiochus's inability to put down the Maccabees was caused by the trouble he had in the East, which prevented him from being involved in Judea himself. Instead, he ordered Lysias, regent of the western part of the empire (Syria), to stop the rebellion and to destroy the Jewish race (1 Macc. 3:32–36; Josephus Ant. xii.7.2 [295f]). Lysias sent a large army under the leadership of Ptolemy, Nicanor, and Gorgias. So confident they were of victory that traders went along to purchase Jewish slaves (1 Macc. 3:38–41). But Judas decisively defeated Gorgias at Emmaus, causing the Syrian soldiers to flee (1 Macc. 4:1–27; Josephus Ant. xii.7.4 [305–312]).

In 164 Lysias made one last attempt against the Jews by personally leading a larger army to attack Jerusalem from the south. Judas, however, completely defeated him in Beth-zur (24 km, 15 mi, S of Jerusalem). Lysias retreated, and Judas marched to Jerusalem and regained all of Jerusalem except the Acra. Having captured the temple mount, he destroyed the altar of the Olympian Zeus, built a new altar, rebuilt the temple, and selected a priest who had remained faithful to Yahweh. Thus on 25 Chislev (Dec. 14) 164, exactly three years after its desecration, the temple was rededicated and the daily sacrifices were restored (1 Macc. 4:36–59; 2 Macc. 10:1–8; Josephus Ant. xii.7.6f [316–326]). This event marked the beginning of the Jewish Feast of Dedication or Lights (Hanukkah). Judas then fortified the Jerusalem walls and the city of Beth-zur. This completed the first phase of the Maccabean struggle. The Maccabees could rejoice, for they had not experienced defeat.

2. Religious Freedom Gained (163 B.C.) Judas's victories made Judah reasonably secure. Two things, however, needed to be accomplished. First, although Judah was reasonably secure, it was felt that all the Jews of Palestine had to be independent from Antiochus's rule. After several campaigns this freedom was won.

Second, the Maccabees wanted to end Syrian control of the Acra in Jerusalem. The Syrian presence was a constant reminder of Antiochus's hellenization program intended to exterminate the Jewish religion. When Judas laid siege to the Acra in the spring or summer of 163, some Syrian soldiers and Hellenistic Jews escaped and went to Antioch for help (1 Macc. 6:18–27).

Antiochus IV died in 163 (Polybius xxxi.9.3f.; Josephus Ant. xii.9.1 [356–59]) and was succeeded by his nine-year-old son Antiochus V Eupator. Just before his death, Antiochus IV had appointed his friend Philip as the regent and guardian over Antiochus V. But Lysias claimed that these privileges had been given to him at an earlier date, and so he crowned Antiochus V (both he and Philip were in Antioch when Antiochus IV died). Because of the troubles in Jerusalem, Lysias with the boy-king went south and defeated Judas at Bethzechariah (18 km, 11 mi, SW of Jerusalem). There Judas's youngest brother Eleazar was killed.

Lysias then laid siege to Jerusalem (1 Macc. 6:28–54). Judas faced severe food shortages (because it was the sabbatical year) and was about to be defeated. Lysias, however, received the news that Philip was marching from Persia to Syria to claim the boy-king Antiochus V and the kingdom; thus he was anxious to make a peace treaty with Judas. Judas agreed to tear down the walls of Jerusalem, and Lysias guaranteed religious freedom to the Jews (1 Macc. 6:55–63). The Jews, however, were still under the Seleucidian rule.

3. Political Freedom Attempted (162–160 B.C.) Having obtained religious freedom, Judas now wanted political freedom. To counteract his drive, the Seleucids strengthened the Hellenistic elements among the Jews. Lysias, it seems, appointed the high priest Alcimus (Jakim or Jehoakim) who, although of Aaronic descent, was ideologically a Hellenist (cf. 1 Macc. 7:14; 2 Macc. 14:3–7; Josephus Ant. xii.9.7 [384–88]; xx.10.3 [235]) and thus unacceptable to Judas.

Meanwhile in Syria, Demetrius I Soter, nephew of Antiochus IV and cousin of Antiochus V, escaped from Rome (where he had gone as a hostage when Antiochus IV had been released), killed both Lysias and Antiochus V, and assumed the throne. He confirmed Alcimus as high priest (162) of Israel and sent him with an army to Judea under his general Bacchides. The Hasidim accepted Alcimus as the high priest probably, it can be conjectured, because he was of Aaronic descent and because the Syrians (or Seleucids) had guaranteed them freedom of worship. Thus the Hasidim broke from Judas's ranks, but they quickly returned when Alcimus, disregarding his promise not to harm them, slew sixty of them (1 Macc. 7:15–20; Josephus Ant. xii.10.2 [393–97]). Hence Alcimus asked Demetrius for more military help against Judas and his followers, called the HASIDEANS (2 Macc. 14:6). Demetrius sent NICANOR, but he was defeated and killed at Adasa (6 km, 4 mi, N of Jerusalem) on 13 Adar (Mar. 9) 161, (which the Jews celebrate annually as Nicanor's Day); the army fled to Gazara (32 km, 20 mi, W of Adasa) and was destroyed. Alcimus fled to Syria (1 Macc. 7:26–50; Josephus Ant. xii.10.3–5 [398–412]).

Judas sent for help from Rome, but before any could arrive, Demetrius sent Bacchides with Alcimus to avenge Nicanor's death. Because of the might of the Syrian army, many deserted Judas, and in the Battle of Elasa (about 16 km, 10 mi, N of Jerusalem) he was slain (160). His brothers Jonathan and Simon took his body to be buried at Modein (1 Macc. 8:1–9:22; Josephus Ant. xii.10.6–11.2 [413–434]).

D. Jonathan (160–143 B.C.) Judas's death was a great blow to morale. The Hellenists were temporarily in control while Jonathan and his followers were in the wilderness of Tekoa, waging only guerrilla warfare. Bacchides fortified Jerusalem and other Judean cities against possible Maccabean attacks. In May, 159 B.C., Alcimus died, and no successor was chosen. Soon after, Bacchides left his command in Judah and returned to Antioch (157); he went back to Jerusalem at the request of the Hellenists but was defeated at Beth-basi (10 km,

6 mi, S of Jerusalem). He made a peace treaty with Jonathan and then returned to Antioch.

This treaty weakened the Hellenists' position. Jonathan made Michmash (14 km, 9 mi, S of Jerusalem) his headquarters, where he judged the people, punishing the hellenizers (1 Macc. 9:23–27; Josephus Ant. xiii.1.1–6 [1–34]). During the next five years his power increased. In 152 he was further helped by internal struggles for power in Syria. A pretender, Alexander Balas, who claimed to be the son of Antiochus Epiphanes, challenged Demetrius I. Both desired Jonathan's support. Fortunately, Jonathan sided with Alexander Balas, for in 150 Demetrius was slain in a battle against Alexander. Alexander made Jonathan a general, governor, and high priest of Judah and considered him one of his chief friends (1 Macc. 10:22–66; Josephus Ant. xiii.2.3f [46–61]; 4.1f [80–85]). This was certainly a strange alliance, i.e., Alexander Balas, professed son of Antiochus Epiphanes, in league with a Maccabean!

New troubles came in Syria. Demetrius's son, Demetrius II Nicator, challenged Alexander Balas in 147 and finally defeated him in 145. Since Demetrius II was only sixteen and inexperienced, Jonathan took the opportunity to attack the Acra in Jerusalem, where the Hellenistic Jews were still in control. Although Demetrius II opposed the attack, he later conceded to Jonathan by confirming his high-priesthood and granting his request for three districts in southern Samaria. Jonathan was not able to conquer the Acra, however.

In 143 Demetrius II's army rebelled, and Diodotus Trypho (a general of Alexander Balas) claimed the Syrian throne (becoming its first non-Seleucid king) in the name of Alexander Balas's son Antiochus VI. Jonathan took advantage of the situation and sided

> with Trypho, who in turn made him civil and religious head of the Jews and his brother Simon head of the military. Trypho, however, fearful of Jonathan's success, deceived him, arranged a meeting with him, and subsequently killed him. Jonathan was buried at Modein (1 Macc. 10:67–13:30; Josephus Ant. xiii.4.3–6.6 [86–212]).
>
> Jonathan was succeeded by Simon, the only remaining son of Mattathias. A new phase of the Maccabean rule had emerged. Although generally speaking one does apply the term "Hasmonean" to the whole of the Maccabean family, it is more specifically applied to the high-priestly house from the time of Simon to Rome's intervention in 63 because in that period the Maccabean dream had finally come true, namely, the Israelites had become an independent nation. Hence the political and religious life was headed by one family or dynasty—the Hasmoneans.[87]

Daniel 11:33-35 Updated American Standard Version (UASV)

33 And those having insight among the people will **impart understanding to the many**; yet they will be made to stumble by sword and by flame, by captivity and by plundering, for some days. 34 Now when they stumble, they will be given a **little help**; and many will join with them by means of smooth speech. 35 And some of those having insight will stumble, in order **to refine, purge and cleanse them** until the time of the end; because it is still to come at the appointed time.

The Jews who believed and knew the Hebrew Scriptures, "imparted understanding to the many," as they

---

[87] H. W. Hoehner, "Maccabees," ed. Geoffrey W Bromiley, *The International Standard Bible Encyclopedia*, Revised (Wm. B. Eerdmans, 1979–1988), 198–199.

also suffered under severe persecution. The vast majority of the Jews, however, would become apostates, falling away or standing off from the truth, while the few Jews committed to the only true God of the Scriptures would receive "little help" from their fellow brothers. Many of the faithful remnant suffered martyrdom. This persecution of God's true followers would carry over into Christianity, or "the time of the end; because it is still to come at the appointed time," that is until the Second Coming of Christ. "The mention of "the end," however, serves as a transition. From verse 36 on, the prophecy leaps the intervening centuries to predict events related to the last generation prior to God's judgment of Gentile power and its rulers—prophecy that has yet to be fulfilled."[88]

---

[88] Walvoord, John. *Daniel* (The John Walvoord Prophecy Commentaries) (Kindle Locations 6307-6309). Moody Publishers.

CHAPTER 6 The Kings of the South and the North

Daniel 11:36-45 (the End Times)

Some information from an earlier chapter is worth repeating as repetition for emphasis.

Daniel 8:17, 19, 26 Updated American Standard Version (UASV)

17 So he came near where I stood. And when he came, I was frightened and fell on my face; but he said to me, "Understand, O son of man, that **the vision is for the time of the end.**" 19 And he said, "Look, I am making known to you what will happen in **the period of the wrath,** for it refers to **the appointed time of the end.** 26 The vision of the evenings and the mornings that has been told is true,[89] but **seal up the vision,**[90] for it refers to **many days from now.**"[91]

"The period of the wrath," has "the basic idea [of] experiencing or expressing intense anger. The word is parallel to *qāṣap*, except that its expression takes a more specific form, especially of denunciation."[92]

Daniel 12:4, 9, 13 Updated American Standard Version (UASV)

4 But as for you, O Daniel, **conceal these words** and **seal up the book** <u>until</u> **the time of the end;** many shall run

---

[89] Lit *truth*; Heb., *'emet*

[90] I.e., keep the vision secret; Heb., *satar*

[91] Lit *for to days many*; I.e., to the distant future

[92] Leon J. Wood, "568 זעם," ed. R. Laird Harris, Gleason L. Archer Jr., and Bruce K. Waltke, *Theological Wordbook of the Old Testament* (Chicago: Moody Press, 1999), 247.

to and fro,[93] and **knowledge will increase.**" ⁹ He said, "Go your way, Daniel, for the words are **shut up** and **sealed until the time of the end.** ¹³ But go your way till the end; and you shall rest and shall stand in your allotted place at **the end of the days.**"

The "time of wrath," connects it to "time of the end," and says: "It refers certainly to God's time of judgment on Israel at the time of Antiochus Epiphanes; but it also refers to God's future time of judgment during the great tribulation, in the last half of which the little horn of Daniel's first vision will bring even worse affliction" (Wood, Daniel, p. 106).

Campbell adds:

> It should also be noted that the expression "time of the end" occurs in Daniel 12:4 where it clearly means the time approaching Christ's Second Coming. The conclusion, then, is that we are to see an Antiochus Epiphanes a dread picture and symbol of Antichrist to come in the end time, or Tribulation" (Campbell, 126).

Kelly, West, Seiss, Pentecost, and Walvoord all support this dual reference approach to our passage. Walvoord says, "The entire chapter is historically filled in Antiochus, but to varying degrees foreshadowing typically the future world ruler who would dominate the situation at the end of the times of the Gentiles (Walvoord, Daniel, p. 196).

Archer, though hesitant, throws his considerable weight with this position as well:

> This interpretation has much to commend it, for Daniel makes clear through the assignment of the symbol of the "little horn" both to Antiochus of Kingdom III and to Antichrist of the

---

[93] I.e. examine the book thoroughly

latter-day phase of Kingdom IV that they bear to each other the relationship of type-antitype. Insofar as Epiphanes prefigured the determined effort to be made by the Beast to destroy the biblical faith, that prophecy that described the career of Antiochus also pertained to "the time of the end." Every type has great relevance for its antitype. But the future dealings of Antichrist can only be conjectured or surmised. Therefore, our discussion will be confined to the established deeds of Antiochus Epiphanes (Archer, p. 106).[94]

Some Bible scholars rightly understand these references to end times, as an increased understanding of the prophecies in the book of Daniel at that times. "Understandably **Daniel** and his immediate readers could not have comprehended all the details of the prophecies given in this book (cf. v. 8). Not until history continued to unfold would many be able to understand these prophetic revelations. But God indicated that an increased understanding of what Daniel had written would come. People today, looking back over history, can see the significance of much of what Daniel predicted. And in **the time of the end** (cf. v. 9, and note "the end" and "the end of the days" in v. 13) the words of this book that have been sealed (kept intact) will be understood by **many** who will seek to gain **knowledge** from it. This will be in the Tribulation (cf. 11:40, "the time of the end"). Even though Daniel's people may not have fully understood this book's prophecies, the predictions did comfort them. They were assured that God will ultimately deliver Israel from the Gentiles and bring her into His covenanted promises."[95]

---

[94] Anders, Max. *Holman Old Testament Commentary - Daniel* (p. 232). B&H Publishing.

[95] J. Dwight Pentecost, "Daniel," in *The Bible Knowledge Commentary: An Exposition of the Scriptures*, ed. J. F. Walvoord and R. B. Zuck, vol. 1 (Wheaton, IL: Victor Books, 1985), 1373.

Daniel 11:36-37 Updated American Standard Version (UASV)

³⁶ "Then the king will **do as he pleases**, and he will exalt and magnify himself above every god and will speak astonishing things against the God of gods; and he will prosper until the indignation is finished, for that which is decreed will be done. ³⁷ He will show no regard for the gods of his fathers or for the desire of women, nor will he show regard for any other god; for he will magnify himself above them all.

We are now leaving the era of the Antiochus' and Ptolemies and leaping to "the time of the end" that was just mentioned in verse 35. Many premillennial eschatologists believe that verses 36-45 are referring to the final antichrist prior to the second coming of Jesus Christ and his millennial kingdom. It is, for this reason, we will add chapters in this publication that identifies the antichrist as well. For now, we are going to quote leading eschatologists who see verses 36-45 in this light.

Stephen R. Miller, whom I have quote generously,

> Scholars are in agreement that the vision up to this point has been concerned with events between the time of Cyrus (in which Daniel lived) and the death of Antiochus IV, but with v. 36 this agreement ends. Although there have been other identifications set forth

---

As to whether the Jews remained God's chosen people after the rejection of Jesus Christ, the Son of God, see this author's CPH Blog article, MODERN ISRAEL IN BIBLE PROPHECY: Are the Natural Jews Today Still God's Chosen People?

https://christianpublishinghouse.co/2017/03/27/modern-israel-in-bible-prophecy-are-the-natural-jews-today-still-gods-chosen-people/

or http://tiny.cc/mdippy

for the "king" of vv. 36–45, there are two principal views today.

Those who adhere to the Maccabean thesis maintain that vv. 36–45 continue to speak of Antiochus IV Epiphanes. However, there are serious problems with this position, not the least of which is the fact that much of the historical data set forth in these verses (even in vv. 36–39) is impossible to harmonize with Antiochus's life. For example, Antiochus did not exalt himself above every god (vv. 36–37), reject "the gods of his fathers," or worship "a god unknown to his fathers" (v. 38); on the contrary, he worshiped the Greek pantheon, even building an altar and offering sacrifices to Zeus in the Jerusalem temple precincts. Daniel also predicted that this king "will come to his end" in Palestine (v. 45), but it is a matter of historical record that Antiochus IV died at Tabae in Persia.

Exegetical necessity requires that 11:36–45 be applied to someone other than Antiochus IV. The context indicates that the ruler now in view will live in the last days, immediately prior to the coming of the Lord. Verse 40 reveals that this king's activities will take place "at the time of the end" (cf. 10:14), and the "time of distress" mentioned in 12:1 is best understood as the same "distress" (the tribulation) predicted by Jesus Christ in Matt 24:21 as occurring immediately before his second advent (Matt 24:29–31; cf. Rev 7:14). But the clearest indication that this "king" will live in the latter days is that the resurrection of the saints will take place immediately after God delivers his people from this evil individual's power (cf. 12:2). Of course, the resurrection

> is an eschatological event. Finally, vv. 36–39 seem to introduce this king as if for the first time.[96]

Gleason L. Archer, whom I have quoted at times,

> With the conclusion of the preceding pericope at v. 35, the predictive material that incontestably applies to the Hellenistic Empires and the contest between the Seleucids and the Jewish patriots ends. This present section (vv. 36–39) contains some features that hardly apply to Antiochus IV, though most of the details could apply to him as well as to his latter-day antitype, "the beast." Both liberal and conservative scholars agree that all of chapter 11 up to this point contains strikingly accurate predictions of the whole sweep of events from the reign of Cyrus (during which Daniel bought his career to a close) to the unsuccessful effort of Antiochus Epiphanes to stamp out the Jewish faith. But the two schools of thought radically differ in the explanation for this phenomenon. Evangelicals find this pattern of prediction and fulfillment compelling evidence of the divine inspiration and authority of the Hebrew Scriptures, since only God could possibly foreknow the future and see to it that his announced plan would be precisely fulfilled (Archer, The Expositor's Bible Commentary, Vol. 7: Daniel and the Minor Prophets 1985, 143)

John Walvoord, whom I have quoted and referred to often,

> Beginning in verse 36, Daniel described events that have never been fulfilled historically.

---

[96] Stephen R. Miller, *Daniel*, vol. 18, The New American Commentary (Nashville: Broadman & Holman Publishers, 1994), 304–305.

Neither Antiochus Epiphanes nor Herod the Great ever sought to "exalt himself and magnify himself above every god." The individual in view is the still-future Antichrist first described in Daniel 7. The expression "the time of the end" (v. 35) marks the sharp break in this prophecy. Up to this point, the prophecy dealing with the Persian and Grecian Empires has been fulfilled minutely and with amazing precision. Now, however, we are in an entirely different situation.[97]

The belief is that verses 36-45 are referring to the final antichrist in the latter part of "the last days," that is, "the time of the end. Therefore, we need to talk about the antichrist briefly here but in-depth in chapters 9-11. We can define the antichrist as anyone, any group, any organization, or any government that is against or instead of Christ, or who mistreat his people. Thus, we are not just looking for one person, one group, one organization, or one power.

> Variations of the expression "do as he pleases" are used of God in 4:35, Persia in 8:4, Alexander the Great in 11:3, and Antiochus III in 11:16. A similar expression, "It prospered in everything it did," was used of Antiochus IV in 8:12. Because of his personal charisma, intelligence, evil character, and political power, Antichrist will arrogantly believe that he can function sufficiently well without God. The passage seems to indicate that Antichrist will be an atheist (cf. 2 Thess 2:4; Rev 13:6), although he evidently will use religion to gain his position of power (cf. Rev 17). Baldwin declares: "So thoroughgoing is his egotism that he has no option but to be an atheist."

---

[97] Walvoord, John. *Daniel* (The John Walvoord Prophecy Commentaries) (Kindle Locations 6319-6324). Moody Publishers.

> "Unheard-of things" is a translation of the Hebrew *niplā'ôt* (from *pālā'*, "be surpassing, extraordinary"; noun, *pele'*, "wonder"), which denotes "astonishing, shocking, or unbelievable things." Antichrist will spew out shockingly blasphemous words against Christ (cf. 7:8, 11, 20, 25; 2 Thess 2:4; Rev 13:5–6).
>
> The phrase "the time of wrath" is a translation of one Hebrew word, *za'am*, a term that usually denotes the wrath of God (cf. Isa 10:25; 26:20; 30:27; Mal 1:4), and that is the meaning here. God's wrath will be poured out upon Antichrist and the whole sinful world in the last days during the tribulation period (cf. 12:1; Matt 24:21–22, 29–31; Rev 6–19). When that period is over, this tyrant's activities will cease. Though Antichrist will be judged, he himself is part of God's judgment upon the wicked (cf. 2 Thess 2:12), for those who reject the truth will believe his lies and follow him to their doom (cf. Rev 16:13–16). When the evil leader has accomplished his purpose, judgment will fall upon him (cf. 7:11, 26; 2 Thess. 2:8; Rev 19:20). Even Antichrist's activities and the tribulation are permitted by the sovereign God to accomplish his purposes.[98]

Regarding the king of the north, the angel added, says "Then the king will do as he pleases, and he will exalt and magnify himself above every god **[refusing to acknowledge the sovereignty of God Almighty]** and will speak astonishing things against the God of gods; and he will prosper until the indignation is finished, for that which is decreed will be done. He will show no regard for the gods of his fathers or for the desire of women, nor will he show regard for any other god; for he will magnify himself above them all."

---

[98] Stephen R. Miller, *Daniel*, vol. 18, The New American Commentary (Nashville: Broadman & Holman Publishers, 1994), 306–307.

Fulfilling these prophetic words, the king of the north "will show no regard for the gods of his fathers," such as the liberal progressive world that we are experiencing today with their communistic attitudes that promote outright atheism. Thus, the king of the north has made a god of himself, 'magnifying himself over everyone.' 'Showing no regard for the desire of women.' Commentators are getting bogged down in trying to identify who these women are. However, it might be best to think of how women were viewed in Bible times, as subservient to pagan husbands and subordinate to Jewish and Christian husbands. Might we look at it as the king of the north 'showing no regard for these women, namely, lands or powers that are subservient and subordinate to the king of the north, "for he will magnify himself above them all." Verse 37 "concludes by again emphasizing the atheistic nature of Antichrist, "Nor will he regard any god, but will exalt himself above them all" (cf. 2 Thess. 2:4). This deluded tyrant will even demand that the earth's inhabitants worship him rather than their deities (cf. Rev 13:12, 14–15)."[99]

Daniel 11:38 Updated American Standard Version (UASV)

[38] But instead he will give glory to the god of fortresses; to a god that his fathers did not know he will give glory by means of gold and silver and precious stones and desirable things.

Going on with the prophecy, the angel said, "he [king of the north] will give glory to the god of fortresses," that is, the king of the north will place his trust in the power of the military. He believes that he can save himself and control the world through his "god" of military prowess, sacrificing great wealth, specifically, "gold and silver and

---

[99] IBID, 307–308.

precious stones and desirable things," on the "god" of military power.

Daniel Walvoord points this out for us,

> Examining all other passages relating to the end time, it becomes evident that the sole confidence of a final world ruler is in military power, personified as "the god of war," or "god of fortresses." In other words, he is a complete materialist in contrast to all previous religions and all previous men who claim divine qualities. This is blasphemy to the ultimate, the exaltation of human power and attainment. He is Satan's masterpiece, a human being who is Satan's substitute for Jesus Christ, hence properly identified as the Antichrist. (Walvoord 2012)

Daniel 11:39 Updated American Standard Version (UASV)

[39] He will act effectively against the most fortified strongholds, along with a foreign god; he will give great honor to those who acknowledge him and will cause them to rule over the many, and he will distribute land for a price.

The king of the north is placing all of his trust his militaristic "foreign god," acting most "effectively," proving that he is the most formidable military power in "the last days." (2 Tim. 3:1) The king of the north "will give great honor to those who acknowledge him," namely, lands or powers that are subservient and subordinate to the king of the north, as verse 37 stated, "he will magnify himself above them all." The king of the north will reward those who support his worldview with political, financial, and even at times military support.

It is now time to identify more specifically but not absolutely who the **king of the north** is. **Remember**, we can define the antichrist as **any**one, **any** group, **any** organization, or **any** government that is *against* or *instead of Christ*, or who mistreat his people. Thus, we are not just looking for one person, one group, one organization, or one power. In 'the time of the end," the latter part of the "last days," we are looking for a **composite power** or **kingdom** (government) made up of various powers or kingdoms. This author would suggest Russia, North Korea, Iran, as well as radical Islam apocalyptic ideology, and especially the socialistic, liberal-progressive worldview of many countries and the press (media) throughout the world. This composite power is a definite threat to Christ and Christianity. For eight years, the composite king of the north, antichrist, had its greatest ally in President Obama, who put the world at risk with his ideologies. He is an antichrist in that he went to war with true conservative Christianity in favor of Islam. Obama was trying to destroy the king of the south from within by weakening the United States of America military, as well as her Judeo-Christian moral values.

Daniel 11:40 Updated American Standard Version (UASV)

⁴⁰ "At the time of the end, the king of the south will attack him, but the king of the north will rush upon him like a whirlwind, with chariots and horsemen, and with many ships; and he will come into countries and will overflow and pass through.

In these "last days" or "time of the end," the **king of the south** for this author is the United States of America and any ally powers. Have we seen the king of the south "attack" the king of the north during "the time of the end"? (Daniel 12:4, 9) In a specific sense, we are really not in the "time of the end" as of yet because that is a brief period, the great tribulation, just before the second coming of Christ. However, there is little doubt that the election of Donald J. Trump as president of the United States has put the king of the south in an attack mode like never before in recent history. Trump is carrying out the office in a far more conservative worldview than anyone had suspected he would. He is restoring the king of the south to its glory as the protector of the world and true Christianity. The king of the north has responded to the Trump presidency like a "whirlwind" both 'militarily' and in message. From day one, Trump has been under attack from every quarter of the world, especially the liberal progressive media.

Daniel 11:41 Updated American Standard Version (UASV)

[41] And he will come into the beautiful land and many will fall victim, but these will escape from his power: Edom and Moab and the foremost of the sons of Ammon.

"He **[the antichrist Obama]** will come into the beautiful land [spiritual domain of Christ's disciples] and many will fall victim [persecution of genuine Christians], but these will escape from his power [harming but by no means stopping their activity, as Trump is elected]."

Daniel 11:42-43 Updated American Standard Version (UASV)

[42] And he will stretch out his hand against countries and the land of Egypt will not escape. [43] And he will rule over the hidden treasures of gold and silver and over all the desirable things of Egypt; and the Libyans and the Ethiopians will be at his steps.

The king of the south, the United States and allies, "Egypt," has not had complete success against the king of the north because there was an antichrist, Obama, weakening her from within. For example, the king of the south was losing a ten-year war against radical Islam and was having her military gutted, as the world viewed the king of the south as weak and despondent. How are we to understand the reference to "the Libyans and the Ethiopians will be at his steps." The "Libyans and the

Ethiopians" were neighbors of the ancient king of the south, Egypt; however, today they can refer to nations or powers follow in step with the composite king of the north. The battle between the king of the south and the king of the north is entering the latter part of the last days.

Daniel 11:44-45 Updated American Standard Version (UASV)

⁴⁴ But reports out of the east and out of the north will disturb him, and he will go out in a great rage to annihilate and to devote many to destruction. ⁴⁵ And he shall pitch his palatial tents between the sea and the glorious holy mountain. Yet he shall come to his end, with none to help him.

In time, the composite king of the north will embark on his final campaign against the king of the south, and in a great rage [he will] annihilate and ... devote many to destruction." It is impossible to know the specific action that the composite king of the north will take. Nevertheless, motivated by "reports out of the east and out of the north [that] will disturb him," the composite king of the north will carry out a campaign of some sort "in a great rage to annihilate and to devote many to destruction." We can infer the campaign is directed at the king of the south and her allies but what "reports" will be the catalyst that will "disturb" the composite king of the north that prompt such an attack is unknowable at this point.

Who is Gog of the Land of Magog Mentioned By Ezekiel the Prophet?

Ezekiel 38:16 Updated American Standard Version (UASV)

¹⁶ and **you will come up against my people** Israel like a cloud covering the land; it will be in the last days, and I will bring you against my land, so that the nations know

me, when I show myself holy through you before their eyes, O Gog!"

So, who is Gog of the land of Magog? Initially, it would seem that the name "Gog" might have been a proper name that over time came to be used as a general title for an enemy of God's people. However, in order for us to answer that question, we need to search through the entire Bible and see who attacks God's people in a major way. The Bible mentions the attack by 'Gog of the land of Magog,' the attack by "the king of the north," and the attack by "the kings of the earth." (Ezekiel 38:2, 10-13; Daniel 11:40, 44, 45; Revelation 17:14; 19:19) These may very well be different attacks against God's people (the Israelites Ezekiel 38:2, 10-13), which culminate into the final attack by the enemies of God right after the end of the Great Tribulation. Jesus Christ at Armageddon saves God's chosen people by destroying Gog of Magog. We know that all of the nations of the earth are enemies of God's people at the time of the final attack at the beginning of the war of Armageddon. (Revelation 16:14, 16) After that, we enter into the literal thousand-year reign of Christ. So, Gog of Magog refers to a composite group of nations at the time of Armageddon that is in opposition to God's people.

Notice what God says about Gog: "You will come from your place out of the remote parts of the **north**, you and many peoples with you, all of them riding on horses, a great assembly and a mighty army." (Ezekiel 38:6, 15) The prophet Daniel who lived at the same time as Ezekiel, had this to say about the king of the north: "But reports out of the east and out of the **north** will disturb him, and he will go out in a great rage to annihilate and to devote many to destruction. And he shall pitch his palatial tents between the sea and the glorious holy mountain. Yet he shall come to his end, with none to help him." (Daniel 11:44-45) Note that this is similar to what the prophet Ezekiel says that Gog will do. – Ezekiel 38:8-12, 16.

What will happen after the final attack of Gog of Magog, the composite nations of the earth, on God's people? Daniel tells us: "Now at that time [at Armageddon] Michael [the archangel, the most powerful angel], the great prince who stands up for the sons of your people, will arise. And there will be a time of distress [the great tribulation] such as never occurred since there was a nation until that time; and at that time your people, everyone who is found written in the book, will be rescued." – Daniel 12:1.

We know that these difficult times for true Christians today will only go from bad to worse. (2 Timothy 3:1-7) However, we have no need to be overly anxious about the coming attacks on God's people. Rather, our focus at present should be on the sanctification of God and to make known his sovereignty to the world. We know that "the Lord knows how to rescue the godly from trials,[100] and to keep the unrighteous under punishment until the day of judgment." (2 Peter 2:9) In the meantime, we want to strengthen our faith so that we may remain steadfast no matter how any future attacks may impact us. We should have a good prayer life, a personal study program, attend Christian meetings faithfully. – Hebrews 6:19; 10:24-25; Psalm 25:21.

While we are on the subject of God of the land of Magog, we might as well address who is Gog **and** Magog of Revelation 20:8. Just as it represented the composite nations who were to attack God's people at the end of the great tribulation that begins Armageddon, here it seems likely that it is referring to all of the people who will attack God's true people with the same hateful vigor at the end of the thousand-year reign of Christ when Satan is let loose

---

[100] Or *temptation*

from the abyss. Just as like God of Magog, Gog and Magog will also be destroyed. – Revelation 19:20, 21; 20:9.

CHAPTER 7 Babylon the Great, the Beast, the Seven Kings, and the Eighth King of Revelation

Revelation 17:1-18 (the Last Days)

Revelation 17:1-2 Updated American Standard Version (UASV)

17 Then one of the seven angels who had the seven bowls came and said to me, "Come, I will show you the judgment of the great prostitute who is seated on many waters, ² with whom the kings of the earth committed acts of immorality, and those who dwell on the earth were made drunk with the wine of her immorality."

Who is this "great prostitute"? We need to note that this prostitute is 'committing acts of immorality with the kings of the earth, meaning she is not another governmental power. "And the kings of the earth, who committed sexual immorality and mourn wail over her when they see the smoke of her burning" (Rev. 18:9-10), also suggesting she is not a political power of any sort. Additionally, "the merchants, who became rich from her, will stand far off in fear of her torment, weeping and mourning," mean that she is not big business either. However, we see that the 'nations were deceived by great prostitute's sorcery.' This suggests some religious aspect, namely, all false religions, with the apostate churches of Christendom taking the lead in the time of the end. Adding support to this is the fact that "Prostitution frequently symbolizes idolatry or religious apostasy (cf. Jer. 3:6–9; Ezek. 16:30ff.; 20:30; Hos. 4:15; 5:3; 6:10; 9:1). Nineveh (Nah. 3:1, 4), Tyre (Is. 23:17), and even Jerusalem (Is.

1:21)."[101] "With the information that this prostitute **sits on many waters**, John may begin to think that she is, in fact, another symbolic figure. The original Babylon lay on the Euphrates River and had devised an elaborate system of irrigation canals (Jer. 51:13). Later in the chapter, these waters are interpreted globally—they are all the peoples and nations of the whole world (v. 15)."[102] "John mentioned Babylon already in 14:8, where he wrote that an angel cried, 'Fallen, fallen is Babylon the Great, which made all the nations drink the wrathful wine of her fornication.' Worldly Babylon should be seen as a universal force of evil that influences the multitudes of humanity to such an extent that the people are desensitized. Babylon is "the archetypal source of every idolatrous manifestation in time and space.'"[103]

Revelation 17:3 Updated American Standard Version (UASV)

³ And he carried me away in the Spirit into a wilderness, and I saw a woman sitting on a scarlet beast that was full of blasphemous names, and it had seven heads and ten horns.

There was an earlier pronouncement of judgment against ancient Babylon that was described as being "against the wilderness of the sea." (Isaiah 21:1, 9) The city of ancient Babylon lay on both sides of the Euphrates River. It had a double system of walls, which surrounded Babylon, making it seemingly making it invincible. So, the warning to ancient Babylon was that regardless of it walls

---

[101] MacArthur, John. The MacArthur Bible Commentary (Kindle Locations 67538-67539). Thomas Nelson.

[102] Kendell H. Easley, *Revelation*, vol. 12, Holman New Testament Commentary (Nashville, TN: Broadman & Holman Publishers, 1998), 305.

[103] Simon J. Kistemaker and William Hendriksen, *Exposition of the Book of Revelation*, vol. 20, New Testament Commentary (Grand Rapids: Baker Book House, 1953–2001), 463.

and it watery defenses, it was going to become lifeless and desolate. Here in Revelation, John is being carried away in his vision to a wilderness to see Babylon the Great and the fate she too was to suffer. She too was going to become desolate and a waste regardless of her being "seated on many waters (all the peoples and nations of the whole world)." (Rev. 18:19, 22, 23) The great prostitute is not alone!

The great prostitute's "position atop the beast is quite fitting to picture the influence of the religious power over the secular leader. The scarlet beast is the same one who emerged out of the sea in 13:1. The earlier passage does not give his color, but it does note his seven heads and ten horns and names of blasphemy."[104] The antichrist(s) (13:1, 4; 14:9; 16:10) is made up of false religion (apostate churches of Christendom) and governments, political powers, which control the world. (v. 16) In Scripture, scarlet is often the color of luxury, splendor, and royalty. Rather than having blasphemous names, like the beast of Revelation 13, on its seven heads only, it is "full of blasphemous names," because of seeing itself as being divine (cf. 13:1; Dan. 7:25; 11:36; 2 Thess. 2:4). The seven heads and ten horns picture the level of the political Antichrist's control. "The relationship between the harlot and the beast has existed throughout human history but will reach its ultimate closeness in the days just before Christ returns. She controls him, but she also is dependent on him as the friction between the two later in chapter 17 will show (17:16)."[105]

Revelation 17:4 Updated American Standard Version (UASV)

4 The woman was clothed in purple and scarlet, and she was adorned with gold and precious stones and pearls,

---

[104] Robert L. Thomas, *Revelation 8-22: An Exegetical Commentary* (Chicago: Moody Publishers, 1995), 285.

[105] IBID., 286.

and she had in her hand a golden cup that was full of detestable things and the unclean things of her sexual immorality.[106]

If someone in the days of the apostle John were wearing both purple and scarlet at the same time, this would suggest great wealth, which can be contrasted with the white garments of moral purity that are worn by the followers of the Lamb. (Rev. 7:9; 19:14; See 1 Tim. 2:9-10) The gold, precious stones and pearls show the brash but wasteful and excessive grandeur of a wealthy whore. Just consider all of the magnificent buildings, rare statues and priceless paintings, incalculable icons, and other religious things, as well as infinite amounts of property and cash, that the apostate churches of Christendom have amassed. The "golden cup that was full of detestable things" may appear splendid on the outside, but its contents are detestable, unclean. (Compare Matt. 23:25-26.) This symbolic golden cup contains all the filthy practices and lies that this great prostitute uses in her seduction of the nations, as she brings them under her spell. Then, there is "he unclean things of her sexual immorality," which is pictorial of her sick adulterous relationship with the political leaders and businesses of the world.

Revelation 17:5 Updated American Standard Version (UASV)

⁵ And on her forehead a name was written, a mystery: "Babylon the great, the mother of prostitutes and of the detestable things of the earth."

Robert L. Thomas writes,

> *Mystērion* in the NT is usually a mystery to be revealed. So here the true character and identity of the

---

[106] **Sexual Immorality**: (Heb. *zanah*; Gr. *porneia*) A general term for immoral sexual acts of any kind: such as adultery, prostitution, sexual relations between people not married to each other, homosexuality, and bestiality. – Num. 25:1; Deut. 22:21; Matt. 5:32; 1 Cor. 5:1.

woman, previously kept concealed, are now objects of clear revelation (Hailey). The word implies a new revelation, not something to be kept hidden. In this case it is the exposing of what is evil about Babylon (Lenski). Subsequent revelation will show her to be a great city (17:18), but also a vast system of idolatry through the centuries that the great city represents (Bullinger). The system had its beginning on the plains of Shinar through the work of Nimrod and will reach its pinnacle there just before the second advent (Bullinger, Seiss). Reports of Babylon's present utter desolation and impossible restoration are radically overstated.

The other question about the syntactical role of *mystērion*, whether it is in apposition to ὄνομα (*onoma*, "name") or part of the inscription on the woman's head is resolvable through a comparison with 14:8 and 18:2. The woman's name is "Babylon the Great," not "Mystery Babylon the Great" (Smith, Walvoord). This along with the fact that *mystērion* seems to have a parenthetical independence here brings a decision favoring the appositional relationship. This gives the sense, "a name written, which is a mystery" (Johnson).

"Babylon the great, the mother of harlots and of the abominations of the earth" (Βαβυλὼν ἡ μεγάλη, ἡ μήτηρ τῶν πορνῶν καὶ τῶν βδελυγμάτων τῆς γῆς [*Babylōn hē megalē, hē mētēr tōn pornōn kai tōn bdelygmatōn tēs gēs*]) is the name that constitutes the mystery. Babylon is a theme in Scripture beginning in Gen. 10:9–10 with its first mention and continuing into these closing chapters of the last book of the Bible. It was a city where false religion began (Gen. 11:1–9) that has continually plagued Israel, the church, and the world (Walvoord). It will once again become the world's leading city religiously as well as commercially and politically as the end draws near. Her role as "the mother of harlots and of the abominations of the earth" makes her the progenitress of everything anti-Christian.

> This includes all false religions, not just those that are Christian in name only, but also everything that is pagan and idolatrous under Satan's control (Seiss). The Genesis 11 passage tells where it all began, with the building of a tower that became a forerunner of the world's idolatrous practices throughout history (Seiss, Walvoord). So the metropolis that functions as headquarters for the beast's empire has a long reputation for its anti-God stance. It is a city, but it is also a vast religious system that stands for everything God does not tolerate.[107]

Revelation 17:6 Updated American Standard Version (UASV)

⁶ And I saw that the woman was drunk with the blood of the holy ones and with the blood of the witnesses of Jesus. Well, on seeing her I was greatly amazed. ⁷ And the angel said to me: "Why is it that you were amazed? I will tell you the mystery of the woman and of the wild beast that is carrying her and that has the seven heads and the ten horns.

The woman is the great prostitute of false religion headed by the apostate churches of Christendom, who has long been "drunk with the blood [persecution] of the holy ones [true genuine Christians] and with the blood of the witnesses of Jesus." The history of the abuses of the apostate churches of Christendom in spilling the blood of true Christians who attempt to maintain a true faith in Jesus Christ is there for all to see, and will only worsen as we close out "the last days" in "the time of the end." The antichrist apostate churches will spill an innumerable amount of blood of Christian martyrs as will also be true

---

[107] Robert L. Thomas, *Revelation 8-22: An Exegetical Commentary* (Chicago: Moody Publishers, 1995), 289–290.

of the martyrs who refuse to worship the beast during the great tribulation.

Why was the apostle John "greatly amazed"? "It may have been the sight of such unrestrained wickedness in the true nature of the woman and God's permitting her to exist (Kiddle). It may have been his inability to grasp the symbolic meaning of what he saw. It may have been the contrast between the splendidly attired woman and beast on the one hand and a city in ruins that he had expected to see (Swete, Ladd). It could have been some combination of these, but whatever it was, it was different from the marveling of the earth-dwellers over the beast in 13:3, because he was not about to become a follower of the beast."[108]

Revelation 17:8 Updated American Standard Version (UASV)

8 "The beast that you saw was, and is not, and is about to come up out of the abyss and go to destruction. And those who dwell on the earth, whose names have not been written in the scroll of life from the founding of the world, will be amazed when they see how the wild beast that was, and is not, and is to come.

Abyss: (Gr. *abussos*) It is a very deep place, which is rendered "the bottomless pit" in some versions (KJV). This is found the NT and refers to a place or condition, where Satan and his demons will be confined for a thousand years. (Rev. 20:1-3) Abaddon rules over the abyss (Rev. 9:11) The beast is of Satan's design and will rise from the abyss in the last days. (Rev. 11:7) The beast will go off into destruction. (Rev 17:8) It is used at times to refer to the grave as well. – Lu 8:31; Rom. 10:7; Rev. 20:3.

Book of Life: (Gr. *biblos tēs zōēs*) In biblical times, cities had a register of names for the citizens living there.

---

[108] IBID, 291.

(See Ps. 69:28; Isa. 4:3) God, figuratively speaking, has been writing names in the "book of life" "from the foundation of the world." (Rev. 17:8) Jesus Christ talked about Abel as living "from the foundation of the world," this would suggest that we are talking about the world of ransomable humankind after the fall. (Lu 11:48-51) Clearly, Abel was the first person to have his name written in the "book of life." The individuals who have their names written in the "book of Life" do not mean they are predestined to eternal life. This is evident from the fact that they can be 'blotted out' of the "book of life." (Ex 32:32-33; Rev. 3:5) Jesus ransom sacrifice alone gets one written in the "book of life," if they accept the Son of God. However, it is remaining faithful to God that keeps them from being 'blotted' out of the "book of life." (Phil. 2:12; Heb. 10:26-27; Jam. 2:14-26) It is only by remaining faithful until the end that one can be retained permanently in the "book of life."–Matt. 214:13; Phil. 4:3; Rev. 20:15.

Revelation 17:9-11 Updated American Standard Version (UASV)

[9] Here is the mind which has wisdom. The seven heads are seven mountains on which the woman sits, [10] and they are seven kings; five have fallen **[Egypt, Assyrian, Babylon, Medo-Persia, and Greece]**, one is **[Rome]**, the other has not yet come **[United States]**; and when he comes, he must remain a little while. [11] And the beast that was, and is not, is also himself an eighth, and is of the seven, and he is going to destruction.

We can conclude that the first wild beast from the sea (vss. 1-10) and the second wild beast from the earth (vss. 11-18) of Revelation 13 represent two governmental powers. The first wild beast "the dragon **[Satan, Rev. 12:3, 9]** gave it his power and his throne and great authority." The second wild beast "exercises all the authority of the first beast on his behalf and compels the earth and those who live on it to worship the first beast." Therefore, these beasts or governmental powers are against Christ. Consequently, they are antichrists.

We must not overreact to this, believing that everyone within the government is somehow a tool, being possessed and used by Satan or his demons. We must realize that God uses the human governments for his own purposes as well. We have seen in the United States of late, what other countries have long known, without the law enforcement, a part of the government, there would be anarchy. Moreover, without the military might of the United States government, the world would be overrun by evil, such as Islam. If there were not legislatures, we would have no laws, which give structure to our human society. Some leaders and governments throughout human history have been used by Satan to try to stop pure worship, but others have protected the rights of its citizens, which include the freedom of worship. (Romans 13:3, 4; Ezra 7:11-27; Acts 13:7) Nevertheless, because of satanic influence and human imperfection, no human society has ever, nor will they ever bring true peace and security.

Because of Satan's influence over human governments, while Christians are to be in subjection to superior authorities (Rom 13:1), this is only as long as they do not ask anything that is in opposition to God's will and purpose. For example, if the government said, "no more evangelizing about the Bible," we would obey God rather than man. – Acts 5:29.

Thomas writes, "The best solution is that the seven kings represent seven literal Gentile kingdoms that follow one another in succession (Walvoord). In Dan. 7:17, 23 kings and kingdoms are interchangeable, showing that a king can stand for the kingdom ruled by that king (Swete, Lee). The seven kingdoms are the seven that dominate world scene throughout human history: Egypt (or Neo-Babylonia, Gen. 10:8–11), Assyria, Babylon, Persia, Greece,

Rome, and the future kingdom of the beast (Seiss, Hailey)."[109]

Revelation 17:12-14 Updated American Standard Version (UASV)

[12] The ten horns which you saw are ten kings who have not yet received a kingdom, but they receive authority as kings with the beast for one hour. [13] These are of one mind,[110] and they hand over their power and authority to the beast. [14] They will make war on the Lamb, and the Lamb will conquer them, for he is Lord of lords and King of kings, and those with him are called and chosen and faithful."

The ten horns represent all the political powers that presently hold power on the world scene, which also support the image of the beast. Walvoord writes, "The final stage of this world empire has a nucleus of ten kings apparently joined in a confederacy represented by the ten horns. In contrast to the seven heads of the beast, these kings do not rule in succession but simultaneously at the end time." He goes on to say, "The ten horns' rule as kings is subject to the beast, and their time in power is brief. They are a phase of the transmission of power from the various kingdoms to that of the beast itself."[111]

Revelation 17:15-17 Updated American Standard Version (UASV)

[15] And he said to me, "The waters that you saw, where the prostitute is seated, are peoples and crowds and nations and tongues.[112] [16] And the ten horns that you saw

---

[109] Robert L. Thomas, *Revelation 8-22: An Exegetical Commentary* (Chicago: Moody Publishers, 1995), 297.

[110] Or *purpose*

[111] Walvoord, John. Revelation (The John Walvoord Prophecy Commentaries) (Kindle Locations 4227-4228). Moody Publishers.

[112] Or *languages*

and the beast, these will hate the prostitute and will make her desolate and naked, and they will eat her flesh and will burn her up with fire. ¹⁷ For God has put it into their hearts to carry out his purpose by being of one mind and handing over their royal power to the beast, until the words of God are fulfilled.

Ancient Babylon heavily relied on her watery defenses, Babylon the Great today also heavily relies on her many "peoples and crowds and nations and tongues." Kendell H. Easley says, "Surprise. We expected the final Antichrist and his federated powers to hate the Lamb, but we could not anticipate that **the beast and the ten horns will hate the prostitute** [world religions with apostate Christendom taking the lead]. This reflects, however, an observation readily verified from history: evil often turns on itself, carrying the seeds of its own defeat. The twentieth century witnessed a striking example: Russian communism, which arose with such promise at the beginning of the century, caved in on itself by the end of the century. Treachery and treason seem always to find a place in world power politics. Whether the three actions are sequential or simultaneous descriptions of the seventh bowl judgment hardly matters. First, they will **bring her to ruin and leave** the woman once decked out in scarlet and rich apparel **naked**, an ironic punishment for a wealthy harlot. Second, **they will eat her flesh**—just as the wicked Jezebel, queen in Samaria, was literally devoured by dogs (1 Kgs. 21:23), a fitting fate for someone who trusted a seven-headed beast. Third, they **will burn her with fire**. This describes suitably the destruction of a wicked city, but was also the punishment of certain whores in the Old Testament (Lev. 21:9)."[113]

---

[113] Kendell H. Easley, *Revelation*, vol. 12, Holman New Testament Commentary (Nashville, TN: Broadman & Holman Publishers, 1998), 313–314.

Revelation 17:18 Updated American Standard Version (UASV)

¹⁸ And the woman whom you saw means the great city that has a kingdom over the kings of the earth."

In short, the antichrist(s) that Satan used to influence the world, the false religions of every sort, especially the apostate churches of Christendom will have control over the earth in the latter part of the last days, the time of the end.

CHAPTER 8 Donald Trump as President of the United States, what Does This Mean for Christians?

In January 2016, prominent evangelical Jerry Falwell Jr compared Trump to Christ, claiming the billionaire property tycoon lived "a life of loving and helping others, as Jesus taught". "You inspire us all," televangelist Pat Robertson told Trump in February 2016. Franklin Graham, son of renowned evangelist Billy Graham, even suggested that "it was the hand of God" that helped Trump defeat Hillary Clinton.[114]

Some Christians have claimed that the United States is found in Bible prophecy as the King of the South in Daniel, one of the seven kings of Revelation 17, or that Donald Trump was elected at the hand of God. Are these interpretations correct? Yes and no. Rather than just blurt out the answer in a very brief manner, let us reason together as we work our way to the answer.

One thing that we will learn from this Andrews' books is this; there are a few things that will build us up spiritually and maintain our strength in these **last days**. Our relationship with fellow Christians, our regular attendance at Christian meetings, and our sharing our faith with others, will strengthen us, make us steadfast. These are provisions of God that will help us to "be strong in the

---

[114] Many white evangelicals stand by Trump because they are ... January 01, 2018

https://www.newstatesman.com/world/2017/12/many-white-evangelicals-stand-trump-because-they-are-more-white-evangelical

Lord and in the strength of his might." (Eph. 6:10) Max Anders comments, saying, "Paul introduces his final subject by urging the Ephesian believers to **be strong in the Lord**. When it comes to spiritual warfare, we cannot be sufficiently strong by ourselves. If we are going to have adequate strength for the spiritual battles of life, it must be the Lord's strength. Only he has the **mighty power** sufficient to win spiritual battles against the demonic enemy."[115] As we **grow in knowledge and understanding**, our chief desire will be to share our faith.

While Jesus was referring to our giving to the poor, we learn an important message from his words, "your Father who sees in secret will reward you." (Matt. 6:4) He is well aware of any difficult times that befall us. Even though God's "throne is in heaven; his own eyes see, his watchful eyes examine the sons of men." (Ps. 11:4) We know that God never has to sleep, so he is ever watchful, having loving interest in the welfare of his people. God "will command his angels concerning you to guard you in all your ways. On their hands they will bear you up, lest you strike your foot against a stone." (Ps. 91:11-12) Steven Lawson writes, "In part, this sovereign guardianship will be carried out by his **angels** whom the Lord will **command** and commission to **guard you in all your ways**. Satan quoted these verses to Christ in his temptation and shrewdly omitted this last phrase, "in all your ways" (Matt. 4:6; Luke 4:10–11). This divine protection extends only to the place of trusting and obeying God. The angels **will lift you up in their hands, so that you will not strike your foot against a stone** (Ps. 34:7)."[116]

---

[115] Max Anders, *Galatians-Colossians*, vol. 8, Holman New Testament Commentary (Nashville, TN: Broadman & Holman Publishers, 1999), 190.

[116] Steven Lawson. *Holman Old Testament Commentary – Psalms 76-150* (Kindle Locations 2561-2564). B&H Publishing Group.

Remember the precious promise that God's eyes "run to and fro throughout the whole earth, to give strong support to **those whose heart is complete toward him**." (2 Chron. 16:9) God is "is the everlasting God, the Creator of the ends of the earth. He does not faint or grow weary; his understanding is unsearchable. He gives power to the tired one, and full might to those lacking strength." (Isa. 40:28-29) Isaiah then promises that those who place their hope in God, they "will regain power; they will soar on wings like eagles; they will run and not grow weary; they will walk and not tire out." (Isa. 40:31) Contentment and peace belong to those, who accept that the Father's power is always available to them, knowing that God is always interested in their best interests. We need to believe that "we know that **all things work together for good** for those who love God, for those who are called according to his purpose." – Romans 8:28.

We need to understand Roman's 8:28 better as it is often misused. Many read into (**eis**egesis) Paul's words that God causes everything to happen both good or bad. This is certainly one reason that the subject of biblical prophecy is very misunderstood, as well as suffering and evil. It is true that nothing happens outside of God's plan for our good. God is responsible for everything, but not always **directly**. If he started the human race, and we end up with what we now have, in essence, he is responsible. Just as parents, who have a child are similarly responsible for the child committing murder 21 years into his life because they procreated and gave birth to the child. The mother and father are **indirectly** responsible. King David commits adultery with Bathsheba and has her husband Uriah killed to cover things up, and impregnates Bathsheba, but the adulterine child, who remains nameless, died. Is God responsible for the death of that child? We can answer yes and no to that question. He is responsible in two ways: **(1)** He created humankind so there would have been no affair, murder, adulterine child if he had not. **(2)** He did not step in and save the child when he had the power to do so. However, he is not **directly** responsible, because he did not make King David and Bathsheba commit the acts that led to the child being born, nor did he bring an illness on the adulterine child, he just did not move in to protect the child, in a time that had a high rate of infant deaths.

God is **indirectly** responsible for **all** things and **directly** responsible for **some** things. When we attribute things to God we need to qualify (i.e., explain) them. Without explaining the **directly** or **indirectly** part of God being responsible, we would be saying God brought about Vlad Dracula, Joseph Stalin, and Adolf Hitler for our good. God is **indirectly** responsible for all events in human history because he allowed sin to enter the world, as opposed to just destroying Satan, Adam, and Eve and starting over. God is directly responsible for many human events because he directly stepped in miraculously and used a group, person, organization, or country to carry out his will and purposes.

God is **indirectly** responsible for Joseph Stalin and Adolf Hitler. God is **directly** responsible for Babylon conquering Jerusalem. God is directly responsible for helping William Tyndale bring us the first printed English translation of the Bible. We can only know afterward (sometimes) if God is directly or indirectly responsible, and then, it is still an educated guess. Overly attributing everything to God without explaining whether he is directly or indirectly responsible is why unbelievers sometimes see Christians as illogical and irrational. A four-year-old child was rescued from a surging river by a priest in 1894. If the child were rescued in the same manner today, the media would quote Christian leaders as saying God used the priest to save the child. However, only afterward do we know that this is not true. Why? Because that four-year-old child, who nearly drowned in that river in 1894 was Adolf Hitler. Hitler being saved by the priest can be **indirectly** attributed to God not **directly**.

The reason people think that God does not care about us is the words of some religious leaders, which have made them, feel this way. When tragedy strikes, what do some pastors and Bible scholars often say? When 9/11 took place, with thousands dying in the twin towers of New York City, many ministers said: "It was God's will. God must have had some good reason for doing this." When religious leaders make such comments or similar ones, they are actually blaming God for the bad things that happened. Yet, the disciple James wrote, "Let no one say when he is tempted, 'I am being tempted by God,' for God cannot be tempted with evil, and he himself tempts no one." (James 1:13) God never **directly** causes what is bad. Indeed, "far be it from God that he should do wickedness, and from the Almighty that he should do wrong." (Job 34:10 God has **allowed** sin, old age, wickedness, suffering, and death to enter humanity after the rebellion by Satan, Adam, and Eve. He did not **cause** Satan to rebel, Eve to eat of the forbidden tree, or Adam to join that rebellion but God had allowed them to exercise the free will that he gave them. God has allowed the United States to exist and carry on as it has. More on this in a moment.

God has allowed wickedness and suffering, old age and death as an object lesson for his creation. What has this object lesson proven? God does not cause evil and suffering. (Rom. 9:14) The fact that God has allowed evil, pain, and suffering have shown that independence from God has not brought about a better world. (Jer. 8:5-6, 9) God's permission of evil, pain, and suffering has also proved that Satan has not been able to turn all humans away from God. (Ex. 9:16; 1 Sam. 12:22; Heb. 12:1) The fact that God has permitted evil, pain, and suffering to continue has provided proof that only God, the Creator, has the capability and the right to rule over humankind for their eternal blessing and happiness. (Eccl. 8:9) Satan has been the god of this world since the sin in Eden (over 6,000 years), and how has that worked out for man, and what has been the result of man's course of independence from God and his rule? – Matthew 4:8-9; John 16:11; 2 Corinthians 4:3-4; 1 John 5:19; Psalm 127:1.

The United States in Bible Prophecy?

1 Timothy 2:1-2 Updated American Standard Version (UASV)

2 First of all, then, **I urge** that entreaties and **prayers**, petitions and thanksgivings, **be made on behalf of** all men, ² **for kings and all who are in high positions**, that **we may lead a peaceful and quiet life**, godly and dignified in every way.

Some would argue that President Donald Trump is no Christian at all and that he is an immoral man in the extreme. We will allow God to judge Donald Trump in his own time. The only conservativism that we need to worry about is conservative Christianity. Conservative Christians should not have voted for Trump because he is a true conservative or because he is a faithful Christian because those things are irrelevant in the scheme of things.

Paul told Timothy that we are to pray for leaders. Why? Paul answers, "that we may lead a peaceful and quiet life, godly and dignified in every way." (1 Tim. 2:1-2) **In other words**, we pray for and vote for the leader that is going to make decisions that will allow us the freedom to carry out our ministry quietly and in peace.

How Do True Conservative Christians View Voting?

While Trump may or may not be a conservative, genuine, Christian by any means (Matt 7:17-18, 21-23), he is adamant about proposing conservative justices on the US Supreme Court, which can protect Christians freedom for decades to come. Christians will not be forced to share in the sins of the world (i.e., make a cake as a bakery for homosexual weddings), they can act on their conscience. Trump is also very serious about protecting America and the rest of the world from Islamic terrorism and Islam's agenda of undermining our Christian nation(s). Trump is also serious about dealing with the illegal immigrants that are costing the nation and being used only for Democratic votes.

However, more importantly, President Trump is rebuilding what Present Obama tore down. President Obama has the **worldview** that the United States was too big and too powerful and had abused its power by victimizing and taking from weaker nations. Therefore, under Obama's twisted reasoning, if the United States was weakened, the other countries could be strengthened, which would then make the world a fairer place, namely, a social justice mentality. President Obama weakened the united states military crippling them from fulfilling one Bible principle. He also very much weakened the moral fabric of the United States by implementing liberal progressive values in place of biblical Judeo-Christian values. The election of Donald J. Trump halted this implemented liberal progressive worldview from taking us down the path that many European countries had long known. This author will now say that in one year Trump has shown himself willing to fulfill Paul's words in two places with Scripture. Again, Paul told Timothy that we are to pray for leaders, so "that we may lead a peaceful and quiet life, godly and dignified in every way." (1 Tim. 2:1-

2) However, President Trump, against all the odds has been carrying out another aspect of God's Word.

Romans 13:1 Updated American Standard Version (UASV)

13 Let every soul[117] be in subjection to the governing authorities. For **there is no authority except by God**, and those that exist have been **placed**[118] **by God.**

Does this verse mean that God has miraculously set up and established every governmental authority since the beginning of man? No, not at all. God is indirectly allowed governments to form, meaning that they serve a purpose by their presence. Many governments make some effort to make laws that protect their public. Some governments abuse their power in the extreme, like Adolf Hitler. Obama abused his power in that he willfully contributed to the United States abandoning their biblical Judeo-Christian values and shift toward the liberal progressive worldview. He also willfully weakened the United States ability to protect the world from existing threats. Governmental authorities exist because God has allowed them to exist. In some cases, some leaders use their power to protect religious freedom and promote a biblical worldview. The United States has protected the world for over a century from wicked nations and other threats, spilling much of their people's blood and treasures. The world has largely been ungrateful. However, this peace that we have had since World War II, has allowed Christian to carry out their evangelism work in relative freedom. – Matthew 24:14; 28:19-20; Acts 1:8.

Trump is finding himself under attack from the liberal, progressive, socialist media, democratic politicians, Hollywood and so many other segments of society. Why?

---

[117] Or *person*

[118] Or *established, instituted*

Because Obama was about building a socialist nation that hated itself and loved other countries more. Now, Trump is rolling that back and making America first. This does not mean that we ignore other countries. Rather it means that we put American conservative values first. It bears repeating as to why we support whichever politician that will give us religious freedom and protect us from enemies. Paul answers, "that we may lead a peaceful and quiet life, godly and dignified in every way." (1 Tim. 2:1-2) In other words, we pray for and vote for the leader that is going to make decisions that will allow us the freedom to carry out our ministry quietly and in peace. If you are spiritually awake and see the battle that is going on, you need to vote Trump into a second term.

We have, but one leader, Jesus Christ, and the United States has been a great tool to protect Christianity for centuries and can do so up unto the great tribulation. We do not know what the future holds in detail, but we do know that a great tribulation is on the horizon and things are going to go from bad to worse. – Matthew 24:21-28; 2 Timothy 3:1-7.

Therefore, let us carry out our ministry because the time is short, and we can use this period of peace wisely. We need to find a way for true Christians to unite under one God, becoming one in doctrine, word, and deed. We need to proclaim the Word of God, teach and make disciples. (Matt 24:14; 28;19; Ac 1:8) Not all so-called Christians are going to survive Christ's return. (Matt 7:21-23, 1 John 2:15-17) Jesus asked, "when I return will I really find the faith." (Lu 18:8) Not at this point and time with our 49,000 different Christian denominations all swearing they are the truth and the way even though they are all divided. Even churches within the same denominations are divided because of autonomy. Christ's second coming will happen in one of two ways.

ONE: Jesus chooses true Christians out of all of these denominations, and the false Christians will hear the words, "'I never knew you; depart from me, you workers of lawlessness.'" (Matt. 7:23)

TWO: Before the end comes one true form of Christianity will develop and all true Christians will see the light and migrate in the name of uniting under the one God. (Ex. 3:12; 19:17; Deut. 4:35; 4:39; Josh. 22:34; 2 Sam. 7:28; 1 Ki 8:60)

For the Christians that voted for Donald Trump and now believe he is not living up to his word, you need to step back and see the big picture. President Trump is battling Satan's world powers from the oval office, and he cannot do it alone. He needs to be voted in again so that he can restore some of what Obama tore down. Imagine yourself trying to alter a country that was turned upside down from within and you have most other countries against you, the liberal media 24/7 attacking you, liberal Hollywood campaigning against you, big business donating money to your enemies, your own conservative party attacking you, you have hundreds of holdovers from liberal progressive Obama's White House throughout the government, no one truly supporting you, how would you implement your campaign promises? He is not a dictator, nor does he have the power to implement many of his promises on his own. He is doing the best job he can under these trying circumstances. We need the extra four years from 2020 to 2024 to undo all the damage Obama has caused. Replace Trump with another lifetime conservative in 2020 will only return the United States to the status quo of politicians doing what they do.

Bibliography

Archer, Gleason L. *A Survey of Old Testament Introduction.* Revised and expanded ed. Chicago: Moody, 2007.

—. *The Expositor's Bible Commentary, Vol. 7: Daniel and the Minor Prophets.* Grand Rapids: Zondervan, 1985.

Arnold, Clinton E. *Zondervan Illustrated Bible Backgrounds Commentary: Matthew, Mark, Luke, vol. 1.* Grand Rapids, MI: Zondervan, 2002.

Arthur, Alexander. *A Critical Commentary on the Book of Daniel.* Edinburgh: Norman MacLeod, 1893.

Auberlen, Carl August. *The Prophecies of Daniel and the Revelations of St. John.* Edinburgh: T. & T. Clark, 1857.

Auchincloss, William Stuart. *The Book of Daniel Unlocked.* New York: Van Nostrand, 1905.

Barker, Kenneth L., and Waylon Bailey. *The New American Commentary: vol. 20, Micah, Nahum, Habakkuk, Zephaniah.* Nashville, TN: Broadman & Holman Publishers, 2001.

Barnes, Albert. *Daniel. Vol. 2. Notes on the Old Testament.* Ed. Robert Few. Grand Rapids: Baker, 1950.

Bauer, Walter. *A Greek-English Lexicon of the New Testament.* William F. Arndt, Theodore Danker, and F. Wilbur Gingrich, trans. and rev., 3rd ed. Chicago: University of Chicago Press, 2000.

Benware, Paul. *Understanding End Times Prophecy.* Chicago: Moody, 2006.

Black, Allen, and Mark C Black. *THE COLLEGE PRESS NIV COMMENTARY 1 & 2 PETER.* Joplin: College Press Publishing Company, 1998.

Blomberg, Craig. *The New American Commentary: Matthew.* Nashville, TN: Broadman & Holman Publishers, 1992.

Brand, Chad, Charles Draper, and England Archie. *Holman Illustrated Bible Dictionary: Revised, Updated and Expanded.* Nashville, TN: Holman, 2003.

Buter, Trent C. *Holman New Testament Commentary: Luke.* Nashville, TN: Broadman & Holman Publishers, 2000.

Campbell, Donald K., and Jeffrey L. gen. eds. Townsend. *A Case for Premillennialism.* Chicago: Moody, 1992.

Chouinard, Larry. *Matthew, The College Press NIV Commentary.* (Joplin, MO: College Press, 1997.

Easley, Kendell H. *Revelation, vol. 12, Holman New Testament Commentary.* Nashville, TN:: Broadman & Holman Publishers, 1998.

Elliott, Charles. *Delineation Of Roman Catholicism: Drawn From The Authentic And Acknowledged Standards Of the Church Of Rome, Volume II.* New York: George Lane, 1941.

Elwell, Walter A. *Baker Encyclopedia of the Bible.* Grand Rapids: Baker Book House, 1988.

Gangel, Kenneth, and Max Anders. *Daniel, vol. 18, Holman Old Testament Commentary.* Nashville, TN: Broadman & Holman Publishers, 2002.

Goldingay, John E. *Word Biblical Commentary Vol. 30, Daniel .* Nashville, TN: Thomas Nelson Inc, 1989.

Kistemaker, Simon J., and William Hendriksen. *Exposition of the Book of Revelation, vol. 20, New Testament Commentary.* Grand Rapids: Baker Book House, 1953–2001.

Larson, Knute. *Holman New Testament Commentary, vol. 9, I & II Thessalonians, I & II Timothy, Titus, Philemon.* Nashville, TN: Broadman & Holman Publishers, 2000.

Longman III, Tremper. *The NIV Application Commentary : Daniel.* Grand Rapids: Zondervan Publishing House, 1999.

MacArthur, John. *Because the Time Is Near.* Chicago: Moody, 2007.

—. *The MacArthur New Testament Commentary: Revelation 1–11.* Chicago: Moody, 1999.

—. *The MacArthur New Testament Commentary: Revelation 12-22.* Chicago: Moody, 2000.

Mangano, Mark. *Esther & Daniel, The College Press NIV Commentary (: , 2001).* Joplin, MO: College Press Pub., 2001.

Miller, Stephen R. *Daniel, vol. 18, The New American Commentary.* Nashville:: Broadman & Holman Publishers, 1994.

Montgomery, James A. *A Critical and Exegetical Commentary on the Book of Daniel (International Critical Commentary Series).* Edinburgh: Bloomsbury T & T Clark, 1926.

Morris, Leon. *The Gospel According to Matthew, The Pillar New Testament Commentary.* Grand Rapids, MI(; Leicester, England: W.B. Eerdmans; Inter-Varsity Press,, 1992.

Pentecost, J. Dwight, and ed. J. F. Walvoord and R. B. Zuck. *"Daniel," in The Bible Knowledge*

Commentary: An Exposition of the Scriptures, vol. 1. Wheaton, IL: Victor Books, 1985.

Ryrie, Charles C. *Basic Theology.* Chicago: Moody, 1999.

—. *Revelation. rev ed.* Chicago: Moody, 1996.

Smith, J. B. *A Revelation of Jesus Christ.* Scottdale, PA: Herald, 1961.

Stein, Robert H. *A Basic Guide to Interpreting the Bible: Playing by the Rules.* Grand Rapids: Baker Books, 1994.

Terry, Milton S. *Biblical Hermeneutics: A Treatise on the Interpretation of the Old and New Testaments.* Grand Rapids: Zondervan, 1883.

Thomas, Robert L. *Revelation 8-22: An Exegetical Commentary.* Chicago: Moody Publishers, 1995.

Vine, W E. *Vine's Expository Dictionary of Old and New Testament Words.* Nashville: Thomas Nelson, 1996.

Walton, John H. *Zondervan Illustrated Bible Backgrounds Commentary (Old Testament): Isaiah, Jeremiah, Lamentations, Ezekiel, Daniel, vol. 4.* Grand Rapids, MI: Zondervan, 2009.

Walvoord, John. *Daniel (The John Walvoord Prophecy Commentaries)*. Chicago: Moody Publishers, 2012.

Weatherly, Jon A. *THE COLLEGE PRESS NIV COMMENTARY: 1 & 2 Thessalonians.* Joplin: College Press Publishing Company, 1996.

Weber, Stuart K. *Holman New Testament Commentary, vol. 1, Matthew.* Nashville, TN: Broadman & Holman Publishers, 2000.

Wilcock, Michael. *The Message of Revelation, The Bible Speaks Today*, ed. John R. W. Stott. Downer Groves, ILL.: InterVarsity, 1975.

Wood, Leon J., R. Laird Harris, Gleason L. Archer Jr., and Bruce K. Waltke. *Theological Wordbook of the Old Testament.* Chicago: Chicago: Moody Press, 199.

Zuck, Roy B. *Basic Bible Interpretation: A Prafctical Guide to Discovering Biblical Truth.* Colorado Springs: David C. Cook, 1991.

www.ingramcontent.com/pod-product-compliance
Lightning Source LLC
Chambersburg PA
CBHW060159050426
42446CB00013B/2907